All at Sea

All at Sea

A collection of marine legal stories

Clive Ward

ADLARD COLES NAUTICAL
London

First published by Adlard Coles Nautical 1993
an imprint of A & C Black (Publishers) Ltd
35 Bedford Row, London WC1R 4JH

Copyright © Clive Ward 1993

First edition 1993

ISBN 0-7136-3753-6

A CIP catalogue record for this book is available
from the British Library.

Typeset in 10/11½pt Baskerville by J W Arrowsmith Ltd

Printed and bound in Great Britain by
J W Arrowsmith Ltd, Bristol, BS3 2NT

Acknowledgements

The following have assisted me considerably in
the writing of this book:

Carolyn Butters
Nicola Ellis
Motor Boat and Yachting
Chris Fairfax
Tony Olsen
Tim Reynolds
Edmund Whelan
Tom Willis

And without my wife's inspiration and assistance,
I am certain this book would never have been published.

Illustrations by Jake Kavanagh.

Contents

Acknowledgements   **v**

Introduction   **viii**

Case 1 **The shifting keel**   **1**
Merchantable quality, exclusion clauses, implied conditions,
buyer's right to reject

Case 2 **Someone else's fault**   **4**
Insurance, betterment, third-party claims

Case 3 **At owner's risk**   **7**
Bailment, negligence, duty of care

Case 4 **The wreckers**   **10**
Salvage and wreck

Case 5 **A touch of class**   **13**
Liability of Classification Societies and their surveyors,
negligent misstatement, duty of care

Case 6 **Price rises**   **18**
Late completion, underestimating cost, making time the
essence of the contract

Case 7 **Just what the customer ordered?**   **21**
Misrepresentation, liability of brokers in private sales

Case 8 **Never mind the quality**   **24**
Rejection, yard's right to re-tender, reasonable delay

Case 9 **Uncollected goods**   **27**
Bailment, marina operator's right to sell a boat

Case 10 **Properly maintained**   **30**
Insurance, identified perils, personal injury claims

Case 11 **A matter of trust**   **33**
Repairer's lien, yard's right to sell a boat

Case 12 **Handle with care**   **36**
Negligence, breach of contract, disagreement between experts

Case 13 **Genuine reason for sale**   **39**
Buying a stolen boat, obtaining good legal title

Case 14 **Escort service**   **42**
Salvage and salvage awards

Case 15 **Who should be the loser?**   **45**
Registration and outstanding encumbrances

Case 16 **Buyer beware**   **48**
Buying a boat from a dealer

Case 17 **Insured peril or fraud?**   51
Insurance – proving your case

Case 18 **It's an ill wind . . .**   55
Insurance – a fraudulent claim

Case 19 **A tangle in Portugal**   58
Establishing where negligence lies

Case 20 **Who is responsible?**   62
Problems with contracts and verbal agreements

Case 21 **VAT trap**   66
VAT – payable or not?

Case 22 **Left high and dry**   69
Your legal rights when a company becomes insolvent

Case 23 **On the rocks**   72
Insurance claim – might it be the owner's liability?

Case 24 **Insurance – don't forget it!**   75
The cost of failing to take out adequate insurance

Case 25 **A question of ownership**   80
Sale and purchase of a boat

Case 26 **Check up on your surveyor**   85
Importance of a qualified surveyor

Case 27 **Contractor or subcontractor?**   90
Problems encountered when the builder has financial
difficulties

Case 28 **Undischarged and undiscovered**   95
How to avoid purchasing a boat with an outstanding debt

Case 29 **Negligence – but whose?**   97
Legal implications in an accident where several parties are
involved

Case 30 **Insured peril or design defect?**   102
Difficulties to be overcome when the supplier goes into
liquidation

Areas of most concern   106
Common problems among boat owners

Some lessons learnt   110
A letter to the author

Piracy by law   119
A letter to the author

Useful addresses   132

Index   133

Introduction

Boating is supposed to be fun, but for some people it can become a nightmare. The sums of money involved are often large, the boats and equipment complex, and the marine environment harsh and unforgiving. Ward & McKenzie's business is sorting out the legal and technical difficulties that this combination can give rise to.

When the first *Points of Law* article appeared in *Motor Boat & Yachting* over two years ago we explained that, although the stories were based on actual cases from our files, we would not be identifying names, places or organisations. 'It is not the intention of the series to pillory individual companies,' we explained, 'but to make readers aware of their legal rights – and responsibilities.' Not to mention the fact that, in many cases, to report the details would be a breach of professional confidence.

There is another reason. A case is built on documented evidence, and the documents in question can run to hundreds of pages. Name the parties, and you have to record every argument put forward by either side in order to be fair to both. It would make awfully dull reading, and the main principles would be lost in a mishmash of secondary considerations.

With each of the cases we have covered, therefore, we have stripped away the side issues and concentrated on the elements of the law that were most pertinent to the final outcome. Between them, the case studies illustrate the most common causes of marine legal wrangles, and may well help you avoid ever becoming involved in one yourself. But if you do get drawn into a dispute, the information should help you decide whether it is worth taking the matter further.

The above mentioned magazine runs a Helpline service (tel: 0202 604690) in relation to various articles that we write, which allows readers to have 10 minutes free initial advice.

Case **1 The shifting keel**

The facts

Not long ago Frank, a client of ours, commissioned a large GRP sailing yacht to be built by a well known boatyard. After completion and the usual sea trials, the vessel left British shores for Antigua. Shortly after her arrival at English Harbour, Frank wrote to us to say that he was far from satisfied with either the performance or the construction of his new yacht.

The problems had started on his passage across the Atlantic to Antigua, when the yacht had taken on a substantial and uncomfortable list to starboard. The crew tried to correct the list by restowing portable gear and transferring as much fuel and water as they could from the starboard to the port tanks, but with limited success.

Measurements in Antigua proved that there was, in fact, a permanent four degree list to starboard. This could only be corrected by leaving the starboard fuel and water tanks empty. Frank brought the yacht back to the builder's yard where, upon arrival, we immediately noticed that she now had a substantial list to port! Furthermore, the topsides' gelcoat looked shabby and her once attractive teak deck had lifted in places.

A full survey revealed that the keel had a two degree bias to port. Further investigations disclosed the reason for this changing list: the port lower hull and bottom had not been allowed to cure properly during construction. Indeed, they were still viscous, allowing substantial movement in the keel.

What the law says

Normally, a buyer will be asked to sign a contract on the yard's standard terms and conditions. Rarely will he study the small print: his eyes are set firmly on his beautiful, and very expensive, new toy – and if he wants to buy the boat, he has to sign the contract, doesn't he? If he reads the small print, though, he might well discover that the seller's potential liability was limited to the extent of the warranties given. Other clauses would endeavour to limit any further liability so far as the law allows.

A new owner who discovers, after delivery, that his shiny acquisition is tarnished by defects would naturally refer the matter back to the yard. Most builders, aware of the need to retain goodwill among their customers, would respond helpfully, but some, as in the present case, might simply point out the warranty clause absolving them of any further responsibility.

However, all is not necessarily lost for the buyer; deep in his contract shines a little ray of hope. This comes from the obligatory reference to the purchaser's statutory rights. The rights referred to are, broadly, those contained in the Sale of Goods legislation and, in particular, the Sale of Goods Act 1979. Like the integrated Europe of 1992, many people have heard about this Act but not many understand what it means. We shall be meeting some of the intricacies and effects of this and other consumer legislation in the following case studies. The present case, though, highlights Section 14 of the Sale of Goods Act 1979 which, while repeating the old *caveat emptor* rule (let the buyer beware), subjects it to certain conditions. These conditions will be implied into certain contracts of sale and require that the goods sold must be of 'merchantable quality' and that they must be reasonably fit for their required purpose.

It is difficult for a seller to get out of these implied conditions by inserting exclusion clauses into the contract, as the exclusion clauses will only stand up if a court considers them to be 'reasonable' in all the circumstances – in particular, considering the relative bargaining position of either party. This requirement of 'reasonableness' is laid down by the Unfair Contract Terms Act 1977. (Incidentally, the protection offered by Section 14 only applies where goods are sold in the course of business, and therefore a sale by one private individual to another would not be covered.)

What is 'merchantable quality'? It implies that the goods in question are fit for the purpose for which such goods are commonly bought, or as fit as it is reasonable to expect given the description applied to them, the price and other relevant circumstances. In other words, if you buy a £50 engine advertised as 'in need of a complete rebuild' you won't be able to complain that it doesn't work. Taking the principle a little further, the implied condition will therefore not apply where the defects complained about have been brought to the buyer's attention before the contract is made, or where the buyer has examined the goods before signing and ought to have noticed the defects in the course of that examination.

The requirement of fitness for purpose means that where a buyer has, expressly or implicitly, made known to the seller the particular purpose for which the goods are being bought, and where he either relies on, or could be expected to rely on, the skill and judgement of the seller, then it will be implied that the goods are reasonably fit for that purpose.

A breach of these implied conditions is a breach of contract. There are two possible remedies under the law: the buyer may (unless the faults are trivial) be entitled to reject the boat and sue for damages to cover the cost of correcting the defects. He may also be able to claim for other expenses that he has incurred as a direct result of that breach. The question of what damages (such as additional out of pocket expenses) may be recoverable in these situations can become quite a complicated matter, and needs careful consideration by the buyer and his advisers.

Rejection of the defective boat is often the preferred choice, but it carries with it a risk. Consumer legislation is generally of great assistance to the buying public, but it can often work against the consumer where rejection is concerned. This is because the law will in many cases tell the unfortunate buyer that by accepting a boat and using it, he has in fact affirmed the contract and lost his right to reject, even though he was not then fully aware of the extent of the defects.

The only way to avoid this trap is to make it clear at the outset that you will not accept anything other than a boat free from defects. If, following this, defects become apparent, you must waste no time in reporting them to the seller, either asking for those defects to be repaired without prejudice to your right to reject or, straightaway, asking for a new boat to be provided.

The verdict

Regrettably, in this case the yard would not alter their view and, after a long and hard battle, the matter went to the High Court. Happily for Frank, the court decided that, as he had immediately notified the yard of the symptoms he had discovered, he had not lost the right to reject. The actual cause proved very difficult to determine, but luckily the court were kind enough to take a practical view of the matter. They decided that he was entitled to the return of his purchase price and recovery of his relevant consequential losses.

Case **2 Someone else's fault**

The facts

A client of ours – let's call him John – anchored his 10-year-old 40 ft motor cruiser in a south coast bay. A large powerboat approached and dropped anchor nearby. On board the powerboat were the owner and his teenage son, and while Dad fiddled with the winch forward his son was left at the controls.

What happened next would send a shudder down the spine of any boat owner. John, enjoying the sun on the aft deck, was torn from his summer's reverie by the realisation that the powerboat had suddenly gone into full astern and was heading straight for him! Within seconds it had collided with the anchored cruiser, causing substantial damage to the topsides.

After the understandable explosion of expletives and, more importantly, an exchange of insurance details, John managed (just) to get his boat to a local boatyard, where it was lifted out. John duly notified his insurance company, who sent along their own loss adjuster to assess the damage. After this had been done, the boatyard quoted the sum of £12,000 for the repairs.

The insurance company agreed to allow the yard in question to carry out the repairs, but told John that he would have to pay up front for the work. Nor were they going to pay the whole £12,000: as well as deducting his £200 excess, they intended to knock another 25 per cent off the settlement to take account of what they called a 'betterment factor'. John was therefore faced with having to pick up a substantial bill, unsure of when he was going to be repaid but knowing that he was going to be short by at least £3,000. He also had to charter a replacement boat to fulfil a holiday obligation.

What the law says

Marine insurance is a complex subject, but the majority of private boat owners will, through a broker, enter into a contract that will almost certainly be based upon standard conditions known as the Institute Yacht Clauses. Of course, a boat owner may vary or add to these standard clauses after negotiation with the insurers concerned. It is worth noting in passing that the interpretation of these standard clauses, and their predecessors, is subject to statute as well as to a substantial body of case law decided by the courts.

This particular case highlights two of the most important principles that a boat owner should bear in mind if he has to make a claim on the policy.

First, the contract of marine insurance is one of indemnity. Therefore the insurer is agreeing to reimburse an owner for the costs of putting right an insured loss. This means that the unfortunate owner has, for example, to pay the yard carrying out the repairs up front and then present the receipted invoice for those repairs to his insurer, through his broker, for settlement. Owners often assume that the insurance for their boat is similar to the insurance they have for their car, and that if a claim arises they simply hand the matter over to the insurance company or underwriter to sort it all out. Sadly, it doesn't work that way.

Secondly, when carrying out repairs to a boat that is anything but brand new the owner may find, as in the present case, that the insurer will refer to one of the exclusions in the policy of insurance, which states that no claim shall be allowed for expenditure incurred by reason of 'betterment'. As the word implies, this simply means that the insurance company will not pay to improve a boat above and beyond its condition at the time the damage occurred. The boat owner may be faced with the apparent paradox of having to pay out a certain sum of money to have his boat repaired, but not being able to obtain 100 per cent recovery from his insurers as the repairs to be carried out will unavoidably result in an element of improvement to the boat.

However, these difficulties do not necessarily mean that the owner will end up out of pocket. In third party claims, damage resulting in financial loss has been caused by the acts of another; so if the wrongdoer has acted negligently, the innocent party will have a claim against him for any losses he has suffered as a result. Assuming that the innocent party is able to prove negligence, he can expect to recover all the losses not covered by his insurance: the portion of the repair costs that have been deducted by reason of betterment and any consequential losses naturally arising from the damage.

Whether negligence can be proved in any given case will be determined according to principles that we will cover in Case 20.

The verdict

Having considered the nature of the damage and the repairs that had to be carried out, John decided not to take issue with his insurers over the question of betterment. Fortunately, he had the resources to put the necessary repairs in hand, for which he was reimbursed the agreed amount by the insurance company on production of the yard's receipted bill.

As to the losses that were not covered by insurance, namely the remaining repair costs and the expense of chartering the substitute boat, a claim founded in negligence was brought against the powerboat owner. A court eventually found in favour of our client, determining that the other party had indeed been negligent in permitting someone who was not reasonably competent to be let loose on the controls of a powerful boat, as a result of which damage to the property of others was not just foreseeable but almost inevitable. John accordingly recovered his losses together with legal costs.

Case **3 At owner's risk**

The facts

This case concerns the unfortunate story of someone we will call Peter, who had taken his large motor sailer to a south coast yard to have certain routine works undertaken prior to her going on charter.

A short while after work started, a large powerboat that had just been re-engined by the same yard was taken out for a trial by the yard engineer. The work on this boat had, however, not been fully completed. On its return, the engineer had some difficulty in manoeuvring the powerboat, which veered out of control and gave Peter's motor sailer a hefty bash.

So severe was the damage caused that the yard only just prevented the motor sailer from sinking and had to lift her ashore. They tried unsuccessfully to contact Peter, who was abroad at the time, and then decided to start repairs on the boat immediately.

When Peter returned to the UK he learned with horror of what had happened to his boat. To rub salt into his already smarting wounds he was also told by the yard that they would not release his vessel until he had paid both for the routine work undertaken by the yard and for the repair work needed after the accident – which came to some £13,000.

Peter settled the invoice for the routine work but, understandably, refused to pay for the repairs. A further blow came when his insurance company wrote to say they were denying all liability for the cost of repairs, as they had been given no opportunity to have their own surveyor inspect the damage.

Not one to be easily beaten, and obviously believing that possession is nine-tenths of the law, Peter carried out an SAS-style mission late one night and removed the vessel from the yard's mooring without their knowledge or consent. The yard reacted by suing Peter for the cost of repairs and placing an arrest warrant on the vessel.

At this point, Peter decided to seek advice. We advised him to defend the yard's claim and to raise a counterclaim, principally based on the yard's negligence in breaching their duty as bailees of the vessel (more on that shortly); in permitting an unfinished, powerful boat to be manoeuvred in close proximity to other vessels under their care; and in failing to notify the owner's insurance company of the damage and the proposed repairs. The principal loss cited in the counterclaim was loss of charter fees while Peter's boat was first being repaired and then under arrest.

What the law says

This case gave rise to a number of interesting points of law and evidence, but for the present purposes we shall restrict our comment to the major issues.

The first of those issues concerns a principle known as bailment. When someone is given the task of looking after your property, the law considers them to be a bailee of that property. A pawnbroker is the bailee of the goods he holds, a yard owner the bailee of the boats at his premises.

The law says that a bailee has a duty to take reasonable care of the property in his possession. If the property is damaged, the bailee can only escape liability if he can prove that the damage arose as a result of an outside factor and that he had not been negligent. The important point to note here is that the burden of proof lies on the bailee, and not upon the person claiming damages for the loss – the reverse of the usual situation outside bailment.

In the present case, the yard said they were not liable as bailees because the damage had not been caused by their carrying out the work scheduled for the motor sailer: instead, the damage was caused by an outside factor – namely the powerboat. They argued that it was therefore up to Peter to prove negligence on their part.

This brings us on to the second main issue highlighted by this case, which is the law of negligence. In legal parlance, negligence is described as a 'tort', a word of Norman French origin that simply means a civil wrong. Other torts include nuisance and trespass. Anyway, back to the tort of negligence. Over hundreds of years and after the flowing of much ink, the courts have teased out a number of requirements that must be satisfied for a claim based in negligence to be founded.

1 A 'duty of care' must exist. Such a duty is owed by a doctor to a patient, a driver to other road users, a boat repairer to a client, or marina owner to a customer.

2 There has to be some careless behaviour by the person against whom the claim is being made: the test applied is to measure that person's behaviour against the standards that would be expected of a reasonable person in those circumstances. If the person whose conduct is in question has special skills or knowledge – such as a boat repairer – then you would ask what a reasonable specialist would have done in the particular circumstances of the case.

3 The damage complained of must have been a foreseeable consequence of the careless conduct in question – for example, an occupier might defend an injured trespasser's claim for negligence on the grounds that the trespasser's presence was not foreseeable.

4 There must be a causal connection between carelessness and damage – this simply means that, to succeed, the claimant must show that the carelessness caused the damage. Where there are several possible causes, this task is not as simple as it sounds.

5 A point tied in with foreseeability and causation; the damage caused must not be too remote. The courts determine how far a wrongdoer will be liable for the consequences of his carelessness, to avoid too extensive a domino effect.

Not all the requirements of negligence will be argued in every case. However, Peter, as well as arguing that the yard were in breach of their duty as bailees, also argued that they had been negligent in permitting a powerful boat to be manoeuvred in close proximity to other vessels when the control of that boat was in doubt as a result of the partial repairs that had been carried out. Therefore the only argument here really concerns the question of careless conduct, as the other requirements of negligence are not at issue. There was obviously a lot of debate – particularly technical – on the question of carelessness.

The verdict

The court agreed with the yard that the damage to the motor sailer had been caused by an outside factor, but felt that this did not affect the yard's status as bailees. As far as the court was concerned, the yard had failed to discharge the burden of proof upon them to show that the damage had not been caused through their negligence. They were therefore found liable to the extent of Peter's losses, namely his loss of charter hire, related consequential losses and costs – and, needless to say, Peter was not required to pay the yard's £13,000 invoice.

Case **4 The wreckers**

The facts

After the great storm of October 1987 I had the task of surveying a number of vessels that had been driven ashore on Hayling Island. Very early one morning, I was aboard a vessel that was precariously balanced across another when I heard voices nearby. I looked up and saw two likely lads armed with crowbars and bolt-croppers apparently breaking into a vessel only a few yards away. A four wheel drive pick-up stood by, its back full of all manner of boat equipment, including sails, radios, binoculars and other such goodies.

I had my camera with me and rapidly exchanged a wide-angle lens for a telephoto. I photographed the truck, making sure I got the number plate, and also the two men busy about their task. I had taken some 20 photographs when one of the men looked up and noticed me. The man jumped off the boat and ran towards me, with the evident intention of separating me from my camera. He had second thoughts when I unfolded to reveal my full 6 ft 8 in frame.

I had the film developed and delivered the photographs to the local police station. The police identified the men through the registration number of their vehicle and called them in for interview, where they started muttering about salvage.

What the law says

The law of salvage is shrouded in myth and antiquity. Ancient it certainly is – the first statute on the subject dates back to the year 1353. Myth, and an element of romance, have certainly grown up around this subject, with mariners over the centuries forming their own ideas on what is right and wrong. The courts have, however, formulated a set of principles to govern claims for salvage at sea. In broad terms, these principles are as follows:

1 The salvage service must be voluntary – ie the salvor should not be under any legal duty to provide the service.
2 The service must be rendered to a 'subject of salvage' – eg vessels, their gear, cargo or wreck.
3 There must be an element of danger to the subject of salvage.
4 The salvage must be successful.

Once these principles have been established, there comes the important question of reward – which was, in the early days of salvage, not money but a portion of the goods saved.

If a suitable reward cannot be agreed between the owner and the salvor, the salvor would make a claim before the relevant court or, more often these days, in arbitration. There is no set formula for arriving at an appropriate reward. The tribunal will consider all the circumstances but will give particular consideration to the degree of success, the amount of danger to both the property saved and the salvors, the time spent in saving the property, the salvors' expenses, the value of the property saved and the salvors' skills. All the factors are then weighed up and an award made, the upper limit of which will be the value of the goods saved.

The term 'salvage' conjures up many images: perhaps most frequently that of a disabled vessel, lashed by wind and wave, being towed to safety by another, maybe after an argument by megaphone as to the terms of the salvage contract. But this case concerns something a little less glamorous, namely the recovery of property washed ashore, which comes under the heading of 'wreck'.

In two rather romantically entitled cases in the 1830s, *Rex* v. *Forty Nine Casks of Brandy* and *Rex* v. *Two Casks of Tallow*, the court held that, to be 'wreck', goods must have touched ground, although not necessarily have been left dry.

Goods that have not touched the ground at the shoreline are classified as either flotsam, jetsam or lagan. Flotsam are goods afloat at sea, jetsam goods are those cast into the sea to lighten the ship in an unsuccessful attempt to save her, and lagan goods are goods that do not float but are marked for later recovery. (A ship that has been permanently abandoned, without any intention on the part of her master or crew to return, is termed a 'derelict'.) In the early days of salvage, there were important reasons to establish which of these strange labels applied, but since the Merchant Shipping Act of 1894 they can all be regarded as wreck once they have hit the shore.

The Act confers wide-ranging powers on Crown Officers known as Receivers of Wreck – usually the local Coastguard or Customs Officer – to deal with wreck. Among the Receiver's interesting powers is his right to use force to suppress 'plunder and disorder' in the case of a vessel that is wrecked, stranded or in distress and that has come under the greedy eye of bounty hunters. In the case of wreck found upon the shore, the Act says that if the finder is the owner of the wreck, he must tell the local Receiver that he has taken possession of it; if he is not the owner, he must deliver the goods to the Receiver as soon as possible.

Failure to comply with these requirements is a criminal offence. It is important for would-be booty gatherers to realise that it is also a criminal offence to keep goods that have been washed ashore from a vessel, or to board a vessel that is wrecked, stranded or in distress without the permission of the master or the agreement of the relevant Receiver.

Once goods are delivered to a Receiver, he has to post details of these goods within 48 hours at the local Customs House. The owner has one year to claim the goods, and may be liable to pay salvage and expense. Unclaimed goods – or the remainder, after deduction of salvage and expenses – go to the Crown.

The outcome

In this case our friends, knowing they'd had their portraits taken, hot-footed it to the local Receiver of Wreck and handed in the goods they had taken. They told the police they had no intention of actually keeping the goods for themselves but were merely saving them from being lost on the next high tide. They intended to claim salvage – a likely story, since the salvors' reward probably wouldn't have been enough to cover the fines for entering and damaging boats without proper authority.

Case **5 A touch of class**

The facts

This is a report on a case recently decided in the High Court. It isn't one of ours, but it has very serious implications for many buyers of second hand yachts and motor cruisers.

The case was brought by Mariola Marine Corporation against Lloyd's Register of Shipping. It is important because it hinged on the question of a Classification Society's liability if they wrongly issue a Classification Certificate that is subsequently relied upon by a purchaser to his cost.

The subject of the case was an 80 ft steel hulled motor yacht, *Morning Watch*, which might be familiar to longstanding readers of *Motor Boat and Yachting* from the many articles written by a previous owner, the late John Marriner.

The value of classification

Before giving you the facts of the case, we should briefly explain the working of Lloyd's Register. Lloyd's Register of Shipping is one of the oldest of Classification Societies. It shares name and roots with Lloyd's of London, the insurance group, but operates entirely independently as a non profitmaking organisation set up to monitor the seaworthiness of individual vessels. The key is the well known +100 A1 classification. Each part of this tag has a particular significance. The '+', actually a Maltese cross symbol, means that the hull and essential machinery have been constructed to Lloyd's Rules, and that Lloyd's surveyors have paid regular visits to the yard during construction to check that this is being done. The '100' indicates the craft's suitability for seagoing service, the 'A' shows that it has been properly maintained, and the '1' that its anchoring and mooring gear meets the requirements.

Once the vessel has been built, Lloyd's Rules require it to be surveyed every two years in order to remain 'within Class'. It is up to the owner to ensure that he keeps the vessel in A1 condition. If he doesn't, the surveyor will refuse to renew the Classification Certificate, and will stipulate the repair work that will have to be carried out to bring the craft back to A1.

Given this background, it is easy to understand why the marine world traditionally places such importance upon a boat being 'within Class': the simple phrase is taken to speak volumes for the condition of the vessel concerned. You only have to thumb through the 'for sale' advertisements in the yachting press to see how many of them proudly boast that a boat is classed as +100 A1 at Lloyd's. It has long been recognised that this is worth money.

The case

Now to the facts of this particular case. An American gentleman had decided to buy *Morning Watch* through a US company, and sent his agent to look her over. To his great good fortune, a Lloyd's surveyor was just giving the yacht its periodical special survey. The surveyor gave the vessel a clean bill of health, confirming its Class as +100 A1. The prospective purchaser was aware of the reputation of Lloyd's and relied upon the Classification Certificate as speaking for her good condition. He bought her.

After delivery, the new owner was horrified to discover that his acquisition had substantial defects, including severe corrosion to some of the steel plating. This would normally be enough on its own to take her well and truly outside Class, but Lloyd's conceded that the repair work could be deferred until the time of the next survey.

This did not help the new owner, whose boat had effectively been devalued at a stroke. Two years down the line, if he wanted *Morning Watch* to be issued with a renewed Classification Certificate, he would have to pay to repair faults that had already been present at the time of purchase.

The owner suggested to Lloyd's that they might like to reimburse him for the substantial repair costs their surveyor's oversight had saddled him with, but they declined the offer, denying responsibility for the man's negligence.

The intrepid purchaser, showing both US frontier spirit and a considerable degree of public conscience, decided to enter the legal arena and thus commenced proceedings against Lloyd's for the recovery of his losses.

The law

In Case 3, we gave a brief review of the law of negligence, and specified a number of elements that must be present for a claim in negligence to be successful. The first and most vital element is that there must be a legal 'duty of care' owed by the wrongdoer to the innocent party – in this case, by Lloyd's Register to the purchaser.

Fine, you say: under what circumstances does a duty of care exist? To this there is no easy answer. The courts have wrestled with the question for many years and, despite valiant attempts to the contrary, have finally conceded that it is not possible to give an all-embracing definition. In each case, therefore, they start by looking at the precedents. If another court has decided in a previous case that a duty of care arose under equivalent circumstances, all well and good; but if no similar case has ever been decided the court will have to consider whether they should create a new duty of care.

In so doing, a court will first ask whether it is in the interests of society for a new duty-of-care situation to arise. If so, it will go on to consider the type of damage complained of, how it arose, and the relationship between wrongdoer and innocent party. It may then decide that the case demands the creation of a new duty of care. As you will see, this exercise occupied much of the judge's time in the case of *Morning Watch*.

These problems aside, the courts tend to have difficulties in cases like this one, where the losses have been purely economic – especially when the loss is simply the failure to make a profit. In cases of physical damage or injury – X hits Y, and the result is Z's worth of damage – their obligations are easily assessed. However, in the present case, where the purchaser was out of pocket as a result of a statement negligently made to him and upon which he relied, things were not so clear cut.

It was only in 1964 that the courts recognised that there may be liability for 'negligent misstatement', and even then they were anxious to restrict the situations in which this liability could arise. They did not want every careless misstatement to result in liability, and they got around this by restricting the duty of care to situations where a 'special relationship' existed between the innocent party and the wrongdoer.

Under this restriction, liability would arise only where the wrongdoer was fully aware of the transaction that the innocent party had in mind and knew that the innocent party would rely on his advice in deciding whether to go ahead with that transaction. Therefore, there would be a duty of care owed to an identifiable innocent party, but not to any member of the public at large who might conceivably come to know of the statement and act upon it to their detriment.

So, at the risk of over simplifying, we can summarise the case put by the purchaser like this:

1 Lloyd's surveyor was negligent in issuing *Morning Watch* with a Classification Certificate.
2 A special relationship existed between the purchaser and the surveyor, because the surveyor knew that the purchaser was relying on the results of his survey.
3 Because of the special relationship, a duty of care existed between surveyor and purchaser.
4 Lloyd's were therefore liable for losses incurred by the purchaser.

The verdict

If you have come to the conclusion that Lloyd's would be liable to our prospective purchaser, then you would differ from the judge who decided the case of *Morning Watch*. He held that Lloyd's did not owe a duty of care to future purchasers of a vessel who were likely to rely upon a pre-purchase Classification Certificate.

The judge admitted that the Classification Certificate should not have been renewed. He admitted that it was foreseeable that a purchaser might rely upon the survey result, but decided that this was not enough to establish liability. He was aware that this case fell within the bounds of negligent misstatement and economic loss: this rang the warning bells and put him on notice that special circumstances should be present to result in liability, but he did not feel that such circumstances existed in this case. He appreciated that parties other than the owners of classified vessels might rely upon a vessel's in-Class status as an assurance that it has been maintained and is in good condition, but he emphasised that the primary purpose of the classification system was to ensure the safety of life and property at sea rather than to protect the economic interests of others.

It is clear that the judge also considered that it would be very bad public policy to find Lloyd's liable in these circumstances, as he feared that it might give rise to vast numbers of claims – not only from owners and prospective purchasers, but from others such as charterers and mortgagees who may also place economic importance upon the vessel being within Class.

Those in the marine industry would probably differ with the judge on his conclusion as to the main purpose of a vessel being within Class. Of course, safety is a major factor – Class is often required also for insurance purposes – but the practical reality is that Class is used to enhance resale value. If not, then why do brokers bother to advertise the fact? Furthermore, the ultimate irony is that Lloyd's themselves openly recognise this economic fact. We quote from their own brochure: 'And in comparison with similar vessels not built to LR's exacting requirements, they command enhanced resale values – a distinct commercial advantage.'

So if the judge had taken a different view on the question of public policy, it would have been quite possible for him to apply the tortuous rules of law at his command to achieve completely the opposite result – although he may have had more difficulty finding in favour of a purchaser who was not on the horizon at the time of the special survey.

The implications

There are those who say that, as a result of this decision, the Lloyd's Classification Certificate is not worth the paper it is written on. Others say it is like the Bank of England having no responsibility to pay the bearer of one of its bank notes. These views can be well understood. The certain implications of the decision are that a purchaser cannot place any reliance whatsoever upon a vessel being within Class. He can only rely upon his own survey.

If this is the case, then it must also follow that those who are selling boats have no cause to place a premium upon the fact that their vessel is within Class. Problems might arise only where a Lloyd's surveyor has been negligent in carrying out a special survey, but the experience of the unfortunate American purchaser is not unique. We know other buyers in a similar situation who will be none too pleased by this decision.

The point is that certainty has been removed from the equation. With no liability, a guarantee is worthless. Lloyd's may well have won this battle, but in so doing they may well have lost the war.

Case **6 Price rises**

The facts

This is the case of Jan, a Norwegian who was on the lookout for a traditional timber motor cruiser up to 45 ft in length. Having contacted a number of brokers he heard of a boat in Britain that he thought would suit him. Jan went to inspect the boat and agreed to purchase her subject to survey. He paid his deposit and appointed a surveyor who reported that this 20-year-old vessel was basically sound apart from a few minor defects. Jan took delivery some three weeks later. As he intended to restore the vessel to its former glory, he had a full schedule of works prepared under supervision of his surveyor.

The work was put out to tender; one estimate stood out above the rest both because the yard concerned had a good reputation for refurbishment of this type of boat and the price was substantially lower than the other quotes. The yard also indicated that the work would be completed by June; this was important to Jan as he had plans for the boat for that season. Although no formal contract with the yard was entered into, Jan agreed that certain stage payments would be made as items of work were completed. Thus the boat was delivered and refurbishment commenced.

Jan asked his surveyor to keep an eye on the progress of the work and let him know if any problems arose. After some six weeks had passed by, it was quite clear that the work had fallen well behind schedule. As Jan had already made some of his stage payments, he decided to let the yard continue although he would not now get his boat in June as expected. In fact, the vessel was finally ready for delivery in September and, although Jan was justifiably annoyed at having missed most of the season, he was somewhat pacified when he saw what a good job the yard had done.

Jan's restrained joy was unfortunately to be short lived. Before launching, Jan was presented with the final account for the work undertaken. This account was in fact approximately three times the estimate he had been quoted and Jan was, to say the least, reluctant to pay. The yard took the view that the vessel's value had been increased by far more than their invoice, which they considered to be perfectly fair, and they only 'allowed' a 10 per cent reduction. They left Jan in no doubt that he would not be able to take his boat anywhere until they had been paid. As Jan was anxious to salvage what he could from the season and take his boat back to Norway, he was over the proverbial barrel. A temporary solution was agreed by which Jan paid the difference between the original quote and the invoice total into an Escrow Account pending the outcome of the argument between himself and the yard, which the yard fortunately agreed could be determined by way of arbitration.

What the law says

Jan's plight is not unusual and highlights two common areas of discontent: namely, the question of the price quoted for work to be undertaken, and that of an agreed completion date. Problems with quotes or estimates are not just the preserve of the marine industry – people are often more aware of these matters in the property market where examples of builders' excesses have been notorious.

However, one major difference between the world of houses and that of boats is that in the former you are likely to find far more detailed contracts that identify the parties' rights and liabilities. Jan's contractual details were minimal. In particular, he did not have a fixed price contract. In other words, the yard were not bound to abide by the price given in their quote which was expressed to be an estimate only. If a fixed price contract can be negotiated, then this benefits an owner such as Jan. If, as the job proceeds, the owner requires further work to be undertaken then this can be agreed at additional cost.

Nevertheless, a yard may not wish to be bound by such a term, particularly where the work concerned is extensive. So if a fixed price is not agreed, what is the owner letting himself in for? Common law imposes an obligation to pay a reasonable sum for work undertaken. Consideration will be made for all the relevant circumstances, one of which will obviously be the actual estimate provided by the yard.

The other vexed problem concerns the question of an agreed completion date. Usually there will be some indication on the part of the yard as to when the job will be completed. If that agreed date is missed then what does the owner do: does he abandon the project altogether, give it to someone else, or give the slack yard more time to complete? The important general principle to bear in mind is that in a private contract (eg if the boat is intended for private use) time is not considered to be the essence of the contract unless it is *expressly* stated to be.

Where time is not of the essence, then the yard or builder has a reasonable time within which to complete the job. In such a case, if he has provided a contractual completion date that is missed, then this may entitle the owner to any damages arising as a result of late completion, but would not entitle him to treat the contract as terminated.

Therefore, if it is vital to the owner to have his boat completed by a particular date, then he should insert a term into the contract stating that time is of the essence and that completion is to be no later than the required date. If that date is missed, then the owner would have the option of terminating the contract and recovering any money paid together with any consequential damages.

If the contract is for a new craft to be built, then we should mention that the BMIF have a standard form agreement that can be used or adapted to suit individual circumstances. In particular, time can be made the essence of this contract and specific mention is made of the possible inclusion of an 'agreed damages clause' which entitles the owner to a fixed sum of money for late delivery, usually expressed to be so much per week. This is a very useful clause as it fixes from the start the damages an owner will receive for late delivery, thus avoiding the often lengthy arguments after the event as to what damage the owner actually suffered. This clause does not *automatically* form a part of the standard contract and it therefore has to be *specifically* included. This is a matter that is often overlooked by eager owners.

Finally, Jan was fortunate enough to persuade the yard to have his dispute determined by arbitration as opposed to court proceedings. Again, the standard BMIF contract provides for disputes to go to arbitration; this is generally a much more advantageous route for both parties. Arbitration is not only speedier than formal court proceedings, but it is also substantially cheaper and more informal.

The verdict

As Jan could not show he had suffered any actual loss in receiving delivery of his boat some three months late and as he had agreed to let the yard continue with the work beyond June, the arbitrator could award him nothing for delayed completion (this is where an agreed damages clause would have been a great help). As to the cost of the works, the arbitrator considered all the relevant invoices and time sheets. He confirmed Jan's view that there had been considerable overcharging and held that Jan should pay only 15 per cent more than the original estimate quoted by the yard.

Case **7 Just what the customer ordered?**

The facts

Jason, an experienced boat handler, wanted to buy a fast offshore sports cruiser for weekend use and for longer holiday trips. Looking around for a suitable boat, his eye was caught by an advertisement placed by a reputable broker. He contacted the broker and expressed an interest.

The broker sent Jason a specification which, among other things, stated that the boat had twin 150 hp diesels, a cruising speed of 28 knots and a total fuel tank capacity of 150 gallons. Everything else being to his satisfaction, Jason concluded the deal and the boat became his.

Jason's pleasure was cut short on his first trip by the discovery that he could not get more than 16 knots out of the boat. He was even more put out when the starboard engine faltered. Investigations revealed that the starboard fuel tank was all but empty, and the port tank was on its last few pints. They only just made it to a local marina to refuel.

Jason returned home and called in a surveyor. The report gave him something of a shock: the capacity of each fuel tank was just 50 gallons, and the engines were 120 hp not 150 hp, so the boat was unlikely ever to be able to go faster than 19 knots. It would be possible to uprate the engines to 150 hp, but this would cost Jason £4,940 including replacing the tanks with two 75 gallon tanks. As Jason still wanted to keep the boat, his next move was to call in a solicitor to see whether he could recover the money.

What the law says

In Case 1, we talked about the terms relating to 'merchantability and fitness for the required purpose' that the Sale of Goods Act 1979 implies into a contract. However, those terms are only implied where one of the parties is acting in the course of business, which, despite appearances, wasn't so in this case.

Jason's purchase actually counted as a sale between two private individuals. A broker acts only as the seller's agent, and Jason's contract was therefore with the seller. This brings a new set of circumstances into play, because there are no 'implied terms' in a sale between private individuals: you either have to consider terms expressed and agreed or call in the law of misrepresentation.

For a claim in misrepresentation to be successful, the seller or his agent will have to be shown to have made a false representation before the contract was entered into. The representation should be fact rather than opinion: but the acid test is whether it would have been reasonable to expect the buyer to rely on the representation rather than use his own judgement. A puffed-up advertisement blurb would not be classified as a representation.

Secondly, it is essential that the representation was one of the inducements that persuaded the buyer to enter into the contract. Therefore, if a buyer honestly admits that he would have bought the goods at the agreed price with or without the false representation, he will have no claim.

The remedies for misrepresentation will depend upon which of three categories recognised by the law it falls into. The first is fraudulent misrepresentation, for which the buyer can rescind (ie revoke) the contract, claim damages or both. The second is negligent misrepresentation, introduced in the Misrepresentation Act 1967, which also gives the buyer the right to rescind, or claim damages, or both, but allows the court to prevent rescission and award further damages instead. The third is innocent misrepresentation, for which generally the remedy is only rescission, subject to the court's discretion under the Act to award damages instead.

Claims based on fraudulent or innocent misrepresentation are rare these days. A buyer will generally want to claim damages as well as, or instead of, rescinding the contract, so innocent misrepresentation is not much use. With fraud, proof is very difficult. The buyer is therefore far better off pursuing a claim in negligent misrepresentation. To prove his claim, he simply has to show that the representation was made and that it was false. It is up to the seller to prove that he had reasonable grounds to believe, and did believe up to the time the contract was made, that his representations were true.

Damages awarded in negligent misrepresentation hinge on the law of negligence. In Case 3 we explained that negligence is known as a 'civil wrong' or 'tort'. In awarding damages in tort, the court will try to put the innocent party in the position he would have been in if the tort had never been committed; with a claim in contract, on the other hand, the court will try to put him in the position he would have been in if the contract had been carried out.

It is this vital distinction that is at the heart of a claim in misrepresentation. Damages awarded for negligent (or fraudulent) misrepresentation are not contractual damages. The court will try to undo the wrong. Therefore, the measure of damages will actually be the difference between the price paid and a fair price for the goods – which may be rather less than the cost of putting those goods into the condition as price for the goods – which may be rather less than the cost of putting those goods into the condition as represented. It is therefore wise at an early stage to compare the price paid with a broker's estimate of the true value.

Having brought the broker back into the picture, we should

briefly comment on his position, as a buyer will often assume he is liable for a misrepresentation. A broker is rarely liable in such circumstances. First, remember he is acting as agent for the seller. Therefore, any representations he makes are those of his principal, the seller. Secondly, unless the representations were patently ludicrous, the broker would most likely be able to show that he had reasonable belief in the truth of the statements. Thirdly, all brokers' particulars carry a general disclaimer in respect of representations made – not always a let out, but the disclaimer may let the broker off the hook if he can show that it was not reasonable for the buyer to rely upon the statements made.

The verdict

Happily, it was only necessary to exchange a couple of letters to satisfy Jason's claim. This was largely through the efforts of the broker who, understandably, was rather embarrassed by the position he found himself in. After some coercion and modest threats to bring legal guns to bear, the broker and seller between them stumped up the funds to cover Jason's modification. This was certainly a case where the buyer shouldn't have believed all he read!

Case **8 Never mind the quality**

The facts

Harry was approaching retirement and had set his heart on spending his twilight years in the South of France. He therefore wanted to buy a boat to take with him. Having looked around for a while he saw his heart's desire at a boat show and asked the exhibitor if a similar boat could be built for him. The standard form of contract was signed and Harry paid his initial instalment. He also made the stage payments provided for in the contract, although he was unable to check on how things were progressing.

Although a completion date had been agreed in the contract, this came and went without any sign of the boat being ready so Harry, becoming nervous, asked the yard what was going on. The yard said that they had experienced a few problems, but that the boat should be ready shortly. Some months past the original completion date, the yard contacted Harry and said that he could now take delivery of his boat on payment of the final instalment. Harry decided to pay a part of that instalment, but retain £5,000 'just in case'.

Despite his eagerness, Harry was cautious. He therefore had a surveyor check the boat over. The surveyor was horrified by what he discovered. Apart from the fact that Harry's original specification had not been adhered to, the standard of workmanship and construction was so poor that the surveyor insisted that he had a liferaft during sea trials! As Harry had paid a very large sum to the yard, he immediately contacted them – armed with his expert's report – and asked for his money back. The yard did not take kindly to this suggestion.

What the law says

The contract for the construction of a boat is a contract for the sale of goods or, rather, an agreement to sell the goods which becomes a contract of sale when certain conditions are satisfied. For example, the usual standard form of contract for the construction of a vessel provides that the buyer gets property to the materials used in the boat's construction as and when those materials are actually used. The Sale of Goods Act 1979, and particularly Section 14, implies certain terms into contracts made between individuals and those acting in the course of business. Those terms require that the goods provided are of merchantable quality and reasonably fit for their required purpose. Harry's boat was not. Harry's yard had also agreed to provide a boat of a certain specification. They had not done so and therefore were also in breach of an express term.

Harry therefore had a choice. He could either reject the boat and claim back the price paid together with certain extra expenses, or he could accept the boat, have work carried out elsewhere to bring her up to standard and specification, and claim the cost of this from the yard as damages.

Of course, Harry was considering his options *before* he actually took delivery of the boat. The crucial date on which to assess whether a boat meets with the implied terms as to merchantable quality and fitness for purpose is the date of delivery. However, the yard had told Harry that the boat was in fact ready for delivery on a particular date on payment of the final instalment. Until then, although Harry owned the boat, the yard had a lien on it which would prevent him taking it away. Given the yard's comments, Harry could rely on their assertion that the boat was supposedly ready for delivery and could point to the defects his surveyor had found that showed she was well below standard.

Harry was in something of a quandary as to what to do. He really wanted nothing more to do with the boat except get rid of her and have his money refunded. However, if the yard were going to argue the point, he was anxious about the boat remaining on their premises awaiting the outcome of litigation. He therefore considered whether to 'accept' the boat, if necessary paying the outstanding money under protest, getting her to neutral territory, then rejecting her and claiming his money back. By doing this, he felt at least the subject matter of the dispute would be preserved.

The Sale of Goods Act says that if a buyer accepts goods then he cannot afterwards reject them, but instead must claim damages for any losses he has suffered. However, the Act also says that a buyer is not deemed to have accepted goods until he has exercised his right to examine them to check that they are in conformity with the contract. Nevertheless, from a practical point of view, it is always a little perilous to accept goods with the intention of subsequently rejecting them, particularly where, as in Harry's case, the surveyor had already alerted him to the problems. This is particularly important as the Act also says that if the buyer has examined the goods before the contract is made, then he cannot rely on defects which that examination revealed or ought to have revealed. In a contract for the construction of a boat, we have referred to the difference between an agreement to sell and a contract for sale. The debate as to when the contract is made is therefore fertile ground for litigation – which, of course, means expense.

In view of these difficulties, Harry's simplest course was to reject the boat and reclaim the price paid with interest and any expenses he had run up in abortively preparing to take delivery. Were he concerned about the safety of the boat pending resolution of any dispute then he could always get an order from the court protecting the boat from interference – remember, he owns it.

If the rejection route is chosen, then something that is not widely remembered is that the yard has a right to cure the defective tender of the boat by making a fresh tender that complies with the express and implied terms of the contract. This is a right that has only developed through court cases as it is not expressly recognised by the Sale of Goods legislation. Therefore, a yard could 'have another go' at putting forward for delivery a boat in proper condition. If it fails to make use of this second chance, then the buyer would rightly be able to say that the yard had repudiated the contract as it had shown its inability to perform under it. The buyer could then claim his money back. When things have reached such a stage, a buyer will often say he does not want the boat because it is now well past the original agreed delivery date.

We have already seen how a yard would have a reasonable time to make delivery unless time had specifically been made the essence of the contract. Therefore a buyer can only reject late delivery where time has been made the essence of the contract or where a 'reasonable time' has elapsed after the contractual delivery date. What is reasonable would depend on the circumstances. Therefore, if the delay is not unreasonable and if time had not been made the essence of the contract, a buyer may find he has to allow some time for the yard to have a go at re-tendering the boat before he can take further action.

The verdict

The yard maintained their stance against Harry for some while. An arbitrator was appointed under the terms of the contract and initial submissions were made. However, after the yard were presented with a comprehensive technical report, their attitude softened and amicable negotiations resulted in agreement to let the yard put right the boat's defects under guidance, after which she was sold and Harry's losses were reimbursed. Harry then took his money and invested it in a well-known make of ready made motor yacht – but only *after* he had taken the precaution of having her properly checked over first!

Case **9 Uncollected goods**

The facts

Most of our case studies so far have looked at the problems that can face the boat owner. In this case study we are turning the tables to look at a case concerning that rather friendless of creatures: the marina operator.

In fact, our story concerns a small company that operates a few berths as a sideline. We'll call it XYZ Marine.

One of XYZ's berths was occupied by an ageing 35 ft motor cruiser whose owner lived in another part of Britain and only rarely visited his boat. Although the owner had been paying his fees and associated costs irregularly, there came a point where substantial arrears had built up.

Requests for payment met with no answer, and eventually letters sent by registered post were returned undelivered. XYZ were unsure as to what to do next. They obviously wanted to recover the money they were owed and also to give the berth to a paying customer, so the answer seemed to be to sell the boat. But were they entitled to? They came to us for advice.

What the law says

Fortunately for XYZ, Parliament has made provision for the circumstances that they faced, in a statute called the Torts (Interference with Goods) Act 1977. Certain sections of this Act set down procedures enabling the XYZs of this world to dispose of uncollected goods. The procedures revolve around the concept of bailment, which we introduced in Case 3.

First, a definition of the terms. The two parties to bailment are the 'bailor' and the 'bailee', a bailor being the owner of the goods that have been left in the care of a bailee. Therefore, XYZ were the bailee of the motor cruiser, the owner was the bailor. The Act allows a bailee to impose an obligation on the bailor to take delivery of the goods or to give instructions as to how they are to be dealt with. The bailee does this by giving notice in writing to the bailor and delivering this to him, leaving it at his last known address, or posting it to that address. The notice must contain certain information including the name and address of the bailee, particulars of the goods and where they are held, as well as confirming that the goods are ready for delivery and specifying any sums of money that are owed to the bailee.

This arrangement works quite well in the case of a pair of shoes left for repair, for example, but is less clear cut when the contract is for storage, as in this case. The owner of the boat could not be required to collect it until the contract was ended, so until XYZ had given him notice that they were terminating the contract they could not serve the collection notice.

The notice requiring the owner to collect his goods is not, however, the most important feature of the Act, which actually gives a bailee the right to sell goods in certain circumstances. If the bailee wishes to sell goods that he has been saddled with, he will have to serve yet another notice, a notice of intention to sell, to the owner. That notice has to contain the same information as the collection notice, as well as confirming the date on which the goods will be sold.

If the bailee is owed money, he must leave at least three months between the date of serving the notice and the date of sale. He should therefore waste no time in getting these procedures under way. Once the time has come for the sale, as long as the bailee is reasonably satisfied that the bailor owns the goods, he can then sell them. The proceeds of the sale, less the amount owed to the bailee and any costs incurred in the sale, will be held for the owner.

If the bailee complies with the requirements of the Act, a third party buying the goods will get good legal title. However, if it turns out that the bailor did not in fact own the goods, the third party would not get good title and would have to return them to the true owner.

With a registered boat, of course, the bailee can get a transcript of the register, which should confirm ownership. XYZ did just this, only to find that the name of their customer did not appear as the owner of the boat! While they suspected that the register had simply not been updated, it nevertheless caused them something of a problem.

In such a case, or where the Act will not let a bailee go through the simple notice procedure because of a possible dispute with the

bailor over the sums due, an application can be made to the court under the Act for the court to authorise the sale. The benefit of this route is that once a sale takes place by authorisation of the court, the third party who purchases the goods unquestionably gets the full title to them.

If an application is to be made to the court, the bailee does not have to go through the notice procedure. Neither does he have to bother with a notice of intention to sell if he has taken 'reasonable' steps to find the owner without success; nevertheless, in such a case, he may feel safer going to the court anyway.

The verdict

Given the evidence about the ownership of the boat that their researches had uncovered, it did not seem a good idea for XYZ to proceed with a sale by the notice procedure. They therefore made an application to court. The court agreed that the absence of the name of the bailor from the transcript of the register was probably because the bailor, for reasons of his own, had decided not to amend the register when he purchased the boat. They therefore authorised the company to sell the boat and to take what was owed to them out of the sale of the proceeds, together with the costs of the sale. The remainder was to be paid into court to be held for the owner – if he ever appeared to collect it!

Case 10 Properly maintained

The facts

Maurice and his wife Janet jointly owned a large motor sailer. Maurice, a structural engineer, and Janet, a professional dancer, escaped from London almost every weekend during the season to go for a cruise. On one occasion they decided to take two friends on a holiday cruise to Brittany. As they left their Solent berth, the weather was fair and the wind was variable, force 2, and Maurice decided that it would be more relaxing to motor with just the mainsail set.

When they were some 20 miles out, the forestay suddenly parted in the upper terminal. The deck-stepped mast fell aft, crushing both the coachroof and Janet's legs. The VHF aerial was rapidly re-rigged and contact was made with the Coastguard.

Soon the welcome sight of a rescue helicopter appeared and Janet was painfully winched, strapped to a stretcher, off the smitten boat. Hospital X-rays soon showed that she had suffered serious fracturing of both legs, and it was clear that Janet would not dance again for a long time. Back on the boat, Maurice and his two friends motored shakily back to their home port. Maurice immediately notified his insurance company, and got an estimate for the repairs to the boat.

Compensation for Janet's dreadful injury, and the possible loss of her career, was more difficult to calculate. In any event, after some correspondence, Maurice's brokers informed him that underwriters were declining to pay his claim. Maurice was told 'the underwriters are not satisfied that the mast and standing rigging had been maintained in a proper and efficient manner'.

Being a structural engineer, Maurice had undertaken all the routine maintenance of the vessel himself and felt he would have some difficulty in proving that the mast and standing rigging had been regularly inspected and maintained – even though he had managed to get some witness statements to show that, on three separate occasions, he had been winched to the masthead to carry out routine inspection and servicing. Unsure as to which way to turn, Maurice sought advice.

What the law says

Maurice's problems really concerned the proper interpretation of his contract of marine insurance. He had two problems to consider: the damage to his boat, and the injuries to his wife.

The starting point in seeing whether a claim can be made under the contract of insurance must be to check whether the damage complained of has been caused by what is known as an insured peril. Most pleasure marine insurance policies will in fact incorporate the standard Institute Yacht Clauses; clause 9 of these standard terms states that loss or damage to the subject matter of the insurance (ie the boat) will be covered if caused by one of the identified perils. It is important to emphasise that a particular peril must itself have *caused* the loss – in other words, if one of the peril situations was present but damage arose through some other excluded means, then there would be no claim.

With regard to the damage to the boat, this had in fact been caused by the failure of the top forestay terminal. However, Maurice had been told that he was not covered by his insurance as underwriters felt that the mast and standing rigging had not been properly maintained. Looking at the 'shopping list' of perils in clause 9, one peril that is covered is where damage to the boat is caused by someone's negligence, *but* making good the damage caused by negligence in maintaining the vessel is excluded. Underwriters had picked on this exclusion because their loss adjuster had suggested that the failure of the forestay terminal might have been the result of the earlier failure of an independent rigger to fasten the terminal properly in the first place.

Therefore, underwriters considered that the claim was being brought under the insured peril of 'the negligence of any person' which enabled them to argue that liability was excluded as a result of Maurice's apparent negligence in failing to properly maintain the mast and rigging. However, it was pointed out to the underwriters that *they* would have to show that Maurice had been negligent. Given the statements that Maurice had obtained, there was really not a shred of evidence to support such an allegation.

Feeling more confident about his position, Maurice then had to consider the rather more difficult position of his wife, who had not only got the roughest end of the incident, but who now had a very substantial personal injury claim – no small part of which was her claim for loss of earnings as a dancer. Maurice had noticed that clause 11 of his insurance policy mentioned that personal injury claims of third parties would be paid by his insurers.

Unfortunately, his hope was short lived. While clause 11 does say that underwriters will indemnify the assured (in this case Maurice) for, among other things, personal injury claims, this will only apply where the assured himself is liable to pay, and has paid, such a claim because of his interest in the insured vessel. As Maurice could successfully argue that he had not been negligent in maintaining the vessel (which gave him a claim for her repair), that deprived his wife from making a claim against him for her injuries, which he could then have passed on to his insurers.

As it appeared likely that the forestay failure had been the result of negligent work by a professional rigger, Janet's only claim was against that rigger, although further investigation showed that the rigger was not insured nor of any financial substance. Janet was therefore faced with the unhappy prospect of having no one to make her claim against.

The verdict

As to Maurice and Janet's boat, the underwriters were finally persuaded that they would be unable to uphold their allegation of negligence as to maintenance, and they therefore agreed to reimburse Maurice for the cost of repairs less a small percentage for betterment. Unfortunately for Janet there were no grounds to pursue recovery of her losses from the marine insurers or the individual whose activities may well have been the cause of the incident. By a further cruel twist of fate it turned out that she had overlooked renewing the accident policy she had taken out in relation to her profession. This meant that she was left without any means of obtaining compensation for her injuries.

Case **11 A matter of trust**

The facts

Jack and his brother own a successful boatyard and hire boat business in East Anglia. This is a family concern that was handed down to them by their father. Apart from the business of hiring out small motor cruisers, they undertake boat repair and refurbishing work. One day Sid turned up with what used to be an extremely attractive 42 ft GRP cruiser. Unfortunately, Sid had misjudged the height of a bridge, which in turn had made a most effective job of removing most of the coachroof and cabin windows.

Jack and his brother looked at the damage and, after a few days, sent a written estimate to Sid for the repair work that included the replacement of the superstructure moulding. Sid accepted the estimate, and paid the yard 25 per cent 'up front' so that the work could be started. After the new moulding had been bonded to the hull, a further 25 per cent of the estimate was required. This was duly paid by Sid.

Sid was a familiar sight around the yard over the repair period, and Sid, Jack and his brother spent several lunchtimes together in the local pub.

The boat was finally finished, almost on schedule, and everybody was delighted with the result. Sid came to collect his boat and was presented with the final invoice for the repair work. Sid explained that he was not in a position at that time to pay the final invoice, as he was still awaiting monies from the sale of an overseas investment. Jack and his brother trusted Sid and allowed him to take the vessel away.

Several months later the whole matter was with Jack's and his

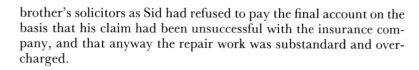

brother's solicitors as Sid had refused to pay the final account on the basis that his claim had been unsuccessful with the insurance company, and that anyway the repair work was substandard and overcharged.

What the law says

The mistake that Jack and his brother made was in allowing Sid to take the cruiser away before he had paid them in full for all the repair work they had carried out. They were too trusting. It is easy to be wise after the event, but they should have insisted upon 'no cash, no splash'.

For a long time common law has recognised that a repairer has a right of lien over goods that are in his possession for the purpose of repair. This lien means that the repairer does not have to release the goods until his bill is paid in full. A shipwright has a lien on his customer's ship, for building or repairing it. An engineer has a lien over his customer's barge, for the cost of putting in the machinery.

For a valid lien to arise, the work must be of repair – not of maintenance. So if Sid's boat had come into the yard for a lick of paint or for her motors to be serviced, Jack's and his brother's rights might have been very different.

A valid lien does not arise unless the work has been completed. The repairer does not have a lien for half a job. If, however, the owner of the item or goods defaults on his contract (eg by not making a stage payment) the repairer is entitled to complete the work and then claim his lien on the completed article.

It is important to note that the lien only arises in respect of the repaired item itself. Had Jack and his brother, by chance, been in possession of Sid's dinghy and outboard, for winter storage for example, they would not have been able to claim a lien on either of those items. The lien they could have claimed (but sadly did not) was only in respect of the cruiser itself.

Another point that may be of interest is that, in these circumstances, a right of lien is not a right of sale. The repairer of an item such as a boat only has the right to sell it if he has expressly reserved that right in his contract of repair with the owner.

In this case, clearly Sid was not acting in good faith; he either did not want to pay, or could not, and so, despite his originally expressed delight with the results of the shipyard's labours, he chose to claim, among other things, that he had been overcharged. As we have seen in previous case studies, it is desirable to have a fixed price contract wherever possible; if Jack and his brother had had one in this case, Sid would not have been able to pull that particular trick and they would have had one less problem in pursuing him for recovery of what was rightfully due to them.

But what if a boat owner (not Sid), acting in good faith, finds that he has been grossly overcharged or that the standard of workmanship in the repairs that have been carried out on his boat is dreadful, or both, but the shipyard will not release the boat to him until the extortionate bill has been paid? Is he really without remedy because of the repairer's lien? No, he can bring proceedings claiming recovery of his boat.

Alternatively, which is more likely to happen, the shipyard sues him; then the boat owner can counterclaim in those proceedings for recovery of the vessel. The court may then order him to pay the amount of the claim into court (and perhaps also a further sum to cover interest and costs). Upon that payment being made, the boat will be restored to the owner.

The action then proceeds in the normal way – ie plaintiff (shipyard) suing defendant (owner) for the money. The only real difference is that the shipyard will, at the end of the day, recover out of the deposited funds the amount to which the court considers it to be entitled. The balance will be returned to the boat owner and the court will make an appropriate order as to interest and costs. What is appropriate will depend on the circumstances of each particular case.

The verdict

Unfortunately Jack and his brother started off with a twofold disadvantage in this instance. They had let the cruiser go and so had no security at all for their claim. Similarly, by doing so they had no means of putting pressure on Sid to be reasonable. They faced the prospect of justifying not only the standard of their workmanship but also the level of their charges, this not being a fixed price contract. They were concerned for their reputation and feared adverse publicity. Worst of all, had Jack and his brother gone to all this trouble and expense and courted the risk of bad publicity, they still did not know whether Sid was worth powder and shot – so the prospects of recovery were far from certain.

They finally reached an out of court settlement with Sid for a fairly small amount, and emerged from the experience sadder but wiser men.

Case **12 Handle with care**

The facts

Sally had just come into some money and decided to buy a new 28 ft express cruiser. On returning from the Channel Islands, she hit some severe weather; soon after this, the inside of the boat started to break up, with cracks appearing on some of the internal mouldings. The galley unit collapsed and the door fell off the loo. Luckily Sally was able to make it back to the mainland, where she had the boat lifted ashore.

A surveyor was instructed and his findings were such that he recommended Sally should put in a claim to her insurance company. The surveyor had discovered that at some time the boat had been dropped while being craned ashore and this, in turn, had broken away the majority of the internal structural mouldings. This accident had not been reported to Sally, and she had collected her boat from the yard not knowing that an accident had occurred. The damage had occurred to the starboard chine, and was not apparent to Sally when she collected the boat after it had been put back in the water.

The insurance company appointed their own surveyor to inspect the damage to the vessel, and his conclusion was that the boat had suffered from misuse while in a seaway, but that the vessel also suffered from latent design and manufacturing defects. The insurance company refused to pay out Sally's claim and suggested that she get in touch with the manufacturer.

The manufacturer replied that they had built 188 boats identical to Sally's and that as none of those had suffered from any latent design or structural defect there was no reason to suppose that Sally's boat was any different. However, they did offer to repair Sally's boat, but for a considerable sum. Sally again contacted her insurance company and asked if there was any way they could claim against the boatyard. They replied that it was not their role to undertake investigations. What can Sally do?

Other investigations

Sally was not prepared to give up, so she took legal advice concerning her position. In the course of discussions, the issues became a little clearer. Her insurance policy contained the usual exclusion against damage resulting from faulty construction or materials, and so Sally's insurers would be entitled to reject a claim if latent design and manufacturing defects could be shown to be the cause of the problem. If this was the case, she might then be able to make a claim against the seller of her yacht under the Sale of Goods Act 1979. This places a legal obligation upon the seller of the boat – who may or may not also be the manufacturer – that the vessel should be reasonably fit for its purpose. In the case of a boat such as Sally's, that obligation would be treated as broken if the boat was not seaworthy and capable of making a passage from the Channel Islands to the mainland in rough conditions.

However, there appeared to be a conflict between the two surveyors' reports. That from the insurance company's surveyor suggested that the damage had been caused by a combination of misuse by Sally and manufacturing defects. Sally's surveyor believed that the damage had been caused largely by the boat having been dropped, and it was pointed out to Sally that the cruiser could have been dropped at the boatyard from where she had first collected it when new – either before she had bought it, or after she had bought it and when it was being put into the water for collection by her. Alternatively, her craft could have been dropped on her return home when the boat was lifted from the water for inspection; in which case, the insurance company's surveyor's own assessment of the cause of the damage would probably have to be accepted.

A private investigator was instructed to make discreet enquiries at the boatyard where the cruiser had been bought. Luck was on Sally's side; the investigator discovered from a disgruntled former employee of the boatyard that a novice crane driver had in fact dropped a boat. He was not able to confirm the exact date or the actual boat involved, but the incident had happened about the time when Sally had bought her cruiser and it had happened to a vessel of similar description. On top of that, the accident described by the former employee would have involved damage to the starboard chine of the boat in question.

Similar investigations at the boatyard where Sally's craft was being inspected after its return from the Channel Islands drew a blank.

To counter the insurance company's surveyor's claim that the vessel had suffered from misuse, Sally was able to persuade her crew to prepare short statements to verify that she had navigated the boat competently and that the weather conditions had not been beyond those that it would be reasonable to expect the boat to cope with.

The verdict

Sally's insurers initially continued to try and rely upon the exclusion in her policy that said that they were not liable for damage caused by faulty construction or materials and that the rest of the damage was a result of Sally's negligence. In the face of the investigator's reports and the statements from the crew, however, their surveyor reinspected Sally's yacht and conceded that the damage could indeed have resulted from the yacht being dropped. The insurance company paid up in full for the cost of the repairs to the boat and are themselves now pursuing a claim against the boatyard from whom Sally bought the vessel for their negligent handling of her cruiser.

Case **13 Genuine reason for sale**

The facts

Geoff saw a postcard in a marina office window advertising a small cruiser called *Giselle*. The advertisement was honest enough to describe the boat as 'in need of some attention', and the asking price of £5,000 seemed to reflect this. Interested, Geoff phoned the number given.

The man who had placed the advertisement, Alan, gave Geoff further details. *Giselle* was basically sound, he said, but could do with some cosmetic improvements. He said he had owned her for four years and was now buying something bigger. In the words of the trade, it seemed a genuine enough reason for sale.

Geoff asked to see the boat. 'Sure,' said Alan, 'it's on a trailer in my drive'. He gave Geoff the address and arranged a time for an inspection. Geoff duly arrived, met Alan on the driveway, looked the boat over, and agreed to buy it for £4,500. Alan even kindly offered to tow the boat to Geoff's home the next day.

Alan arrived as promised with *Giselle* in tow, and Geoff handed over a banker's draft in exchange for a receipt. *Giselle* was his first boat, and he did not waste much time before enthusiastically setting to work on the necessary improvements.

A few months later, Geoff answered the door to two policemen. On passing Geoff's driveway, a man whose boat had been stolen some time before had recognised *Giselle* as being his vessel and had reported the matter to the police. Not surprisingly, the police were anxious to get an explanation as to how *Giselle* had come into Geoff's possession.

A bewildered Geoff explained what had happened, showing them the receipt he had been given and describing Alan. Fortunately, his eagerness to help convinced the police that he was an honest dupe. The police reported back to the true owner, Eric, who contacted Geoff and said that he would like to have his boat back. What was Geoff to do?

What the law says

The general rule in English law is that no one can transfer a better title to goods than he himself possesses, or *nemo dat quod non habet*. This is a very old principle that, in part, has now been included in Section 21(1) of the Sale of Goods Act 1979. What it means is that someone who does not legally own goods cannot give the rights of legal ownership to a third party by selling those goods to him.

In Geoff's case, it was clear that Alan had stolen Eric's boat and sold it to Geoff by pretending that he was the owner and that he had the right to sell her. To add credibility to his ploy, Alan had arranged for Geoff to inspect *Giselle* on the driveway of an unoccupied house that Geoff naturally assumed was Alan's own home. Geoff soon discovered that that was not the case.

The fact that *Giselle* was unregistered did not help matters, but then boats of her size rarely are: if they are registered it is likely to be on the Small Ships Register, which relies on a voluntary and unverifiable statement of ownership and therefore does not constitute proof of title. Only registration under Part 1 of the Merchant Shipping Act provides proof of ownership, which is why finance companies offering marine mortgages secured on the boat insist on it – they can record their interest in the boat on the official register.

Therefore, even though he had paid a fair price for *Giselle*, Geoff did not own her – because Alan had no right to sell the boat to him.

There are exceptions to the general rule. One is provided by Section 22(1) of the Sale of Goods Act 1979, which says that where goods are sold 'in market overt' the buyer gets good legal title as long as he buys the goods in good faith and has no reason to suspect that the seller has no right to sell them. The term 'market overt' restricts this exception to goods bought in shops within the City of London or markets and fairs, and there is a further requirement: the goods bought must be those that would usually be traded there. So clearly, this was no help to Geoff.

A further exception is where the true owner of the goods, by negligence or otherwise, somehow gives the buyer the impression that the seller either owned or had the right to sell them. Again, this didn't apply in Geoff's case.

Eric's position, on the other hand, was cast iron. A bona fide owner who has had goods illegally taken from him is perfectly entitled simply to go and take them back. If the buyer is unwilling to hand the goods over, it may be difficult to do this without risking an action for trespass or damage to property, in which case a safer route might be for the owner to bring the matter to court. The appropriate course would be an action under the Torts (Interference with Goods) Act 1977 for the return of his goods. The owner might also claim damages for their detention.

So poor old Geoff was faced not only with the realisation that he had given his money to a fraudster, but also with the prospect of being sued himself if he did not give the boat back to Eric.

Geoff's only consolation was that, although he had obviously lost the £4,500 purchase price, he need not necessarily lose the £2,000 he had spent on improvements. Section 6(1) of the Torts (Interference with Goods) Act 1977 says that the court can award someone in Geoff's position an allowance for the costs of improvement if he acted in the mistaken but honest belief that he had good legal title to the goods. Geoff was therefore eligible for at least some compensation for the work he had done on *Giselle*.

CAUGHT HIM RED HANDED, TOO!

The verdict

Geoff had no option but to return *Giselle* to Eric, to avoid being faced with further costs. However, it only took a little persuasion to get Eric to recognise the value of Geoff's improvements to the boat and to agree to pay him for the work undertaken. In the meantime, the police tried their best to track down the villain Alan, but to date Geoff has heard nothing of Alan or his £4,500.

Case **14 Escort service**

The facts

The 70 ft motor sailer *Daphne* was making her maiden voyage from
Gosport to St Helier via the Alderney Race. With her owner, David,
and a crew of five on board, she was making good time under sail as
she passed Cap de la Hague.

At about 16.30 *Daphne* passed close to *Perdu*, a 40 ft French-
registered motor cruiser. *Perdu* seemed to be navigating erratically,
and her anchor was partially lowered and trailing astern.

The wind, a northerly force 6, was getting up. Aboard *Daphne*,
David concluded that *Perdu* was probably in distress. He tried to
raise her skipper on the VHF several times without success, then
closed with her and tried again. Eventually he established radio
contact, and discovered that *Perdu* was manned by a crew of only
one, a Frenchman called Pierre. Pierre said that he was in need of
assistance. He had been at the helm for twelve hours and was close
to exhaustion. David offered to escort him to the nearest safe haven,
on Alderney. At about 19.00 the two vessels reached Braye Harbour, and *Daphne* dropped anchor.

Pierre seemed unable to anchor his vessel properly, so two of
David's crew went over to *Perdu* by dinghy to help. Once aboard,
the two crewmen discovered that Pierre was not an experienced
sailor. It also became clear that he had stolen the vessel. He also
told them that if *Daphne* had not come to his assistance he would
have attempted to beach the motor cruiser.

By midnight it was blowing a full gale from the north-east.
Despite the conditions, David decided to visit *Perdu* to check that
she was safe. His inspection indicated that her anchor was holding,
but during the visit he injured a finger.

The next morning David and two of his crew went across to *Perdu*
again, this time to prepare her for a trip back to her port of registry,
Cherbourg. The task completed, David and one of his crew
returned to *Daphne*, but in the heavy swell David was thrown out of
the dinghy. He was recovered without serious injury, but they
decided to wait a while before setting off.

By 15.00 the wind had moderated to force 4/5. The two vessels
raised anchor and began the passage to Cherbourg, with one of
David's crew navigating *Perdu* and *Daphne* standing by to provide
assistance if required. They reached Cherbourg safely at 19.30.
David gave *Perdu* back to her delighted owner and handed a
decidedly undelighted Pierre over to the police.

Once he had started to relax, David reflected on his injury and
exhaustion, the disruption of his maiden voyage and the danger in
which he, his crew and his vessel had been placed. He thought
about making a salvage claim, as some form of compensation.

What the law says

In law, 'salvage' is an action taken to preserve a vessel that is in danger of loss or damage. Anyone who completes or 'meritoriously contributes' to the completion of a successful salvage is entitled to be paid for his or her services. The amount of pay, which is usually awarded by an arbitrator, will depend upon four factors:

1 The degree of danger from which the vessel is 'salved'.
2 The nature and extent of the services provided.
3 The status of the salvors.
4 The size of the salved fund – in this case, the value of *Perdu*.

The last two were simple to establish. The status of David and his crew was that of willing non-professionals, and the value of *Perdu* upon arrival at Cherbourg was put at about £150,000. The degree of danger and the nature of the services provided were more difficult to assess.

When *Daphne* came upon *Perdu*, the latter was about 5 miles off the French coast. The wind was northerly so there was no real danger of *Perdu* being driven ashore in the near future; although she was in the hands of a tired and inexperienced sailor, there was a good chance that she would have ridden out the bad weather without sustaining serious physical damage.

There was some risk of damage from the anchor cable that *Perdu* was dragging astern. In the swell, the cable might well have damaged the hull. But, more importantly, Pierre had said that if *Daphne* hadn't come along he would have attempted to beach *Perdu*. Had he done this in the prevailing wind and swell, she would have sustained considerable damage.

In assessing the degree of danger facing the vessel, the arbitrator will also take into account the possibility of assistance from another quarter. But in this case no other vessels were around, and the difficulty David had in raising Pierre on the radio made it unlikely that he would have known how to summon assistance. So if *Daphne* had not happened on the scene, *Perdu* would have been beached as intended.

The salvage services were provided without hesitation and were efficiently carried out. *Daphne* was in some danger at the beginning of the episode when she closed with *Perdu* in an attempt to communicate with her. Similarly, once at Alderney, the prevailing wind and swell conditions created some danger for those who went across to *Perdu*, amply illustrated when David was thrown out of the dinghy and also when he injured his finger.

Having said that, the services actually provided were of a limited nature, lasting for just over a day. The tasks performed by David's crew consisted of escorting *Perdu* to Alderney and later to Cherbourg; anchoring *Perdu* at Alderney and thereafter maintaining anchor watches; and providing the labour to navigate *Perdu* from Alderney to Cherbourg. The distances involved were modest, and *Daphne* was not at any time required to tow *Perdu*.

The verdict

Although the salvage services provided by *Daphne* were of a relatively modest nature and were provided by non-professionals, there were several enhancing features, such as:

1 Pierre's stated intention to beach *Perdu*, which created a situation of significant danger.
2 The absence of alternative assistance.
3 The fact that the services involved a degree of physical risk to David and his vessel.
4 The fact that the action of those on board *Daphne* restored possession of *Perdu* to her true owner.
5 David's meticulously maintained log, which enabled all the facts to be established with total accuracy and without fear of contradiction.

David's claim never came to court. After some haggling, his legal advisers and *Perdu*'s insurers concluded that the Lloyd's arbitrator was likely to award around £20,000 and they agreed on that as a satisfactory settlement.

There are two points worth bearing in mind: the law of salvage is complex and highly specialised, and salvaging is nearly always dangerous. Do not undertake it if you do not have a full, able-bodied, experienced crew. Instead, put out a PAN PAN or, depending upon the gravity of the situation, a MAYDAY call.

Case 15 Who should be the loser?

The facts

Charles was an avid reader of yachting magazines, so when he saw a privately advertised 35 ft motor cruiser he liked, at a price he could afford, he knew what to do.

First, he instructed a surveyor, who gave the boat a clean bill of health. Secondly, he investigated title. He asked to see the original bill of sale, which was duly produced and confirmed that the vendor had bought the boat, *Geraldine X*, some five years previously. *Geraldine X* carried a Small Ships Register number but no official number, and the vendor said that he had never bothered to go for full registration – in other words, to register her under Part 1 of the Merchant Shipping Act.

Nevertheless, just to be on the safe side, Charles rang up the General Register of Ships in Cardiff to see if they had her on file. He knew that if there was a loan outstanding on the boat, the finance company would have insisted on her being registered under Part 1. After several transfers from one department to another, Charles found a helpful lady who confirmed that there was no entry for *Geraldine X*.

Charles went ahead and bought the boat, borrowing the money against the security of his own house. Four months later, he went down to the boat to find a writ taped to the saloon door. It said that the Easy Finance Company (EFC) had an undischarged interest in *Geraldine X*, and it threatened him with all sorts of legal proceedings if he laid a finger on her. The writ, however, quoted the name of the boat as *Paragon*, so he phoned EFC to tell them they had made a mistake.

Not so, said EFC's credit controller. Their client – the man who sold Charles the boat – had changed her name to *Paragon* last year and registered her in that name before they lent him the money. Deliberately, presumably, he had never put up the official number or changed the name on the stern.

So chase *him* for the money, said Charles. EFC admitted they didn't know where he was. So would Charles please either take over the payments or sell *Geraldine X/Paragon* and give them the £25,000? When Charles had picked himself up off the floor, he phoned us.

What the law says

There had clearly been a fraud perpetrated on both EFC and Charles. In the absence of the seller (who, not surprisingly, had disappeared to sunnier climes), one of them had to be the loser and the question was which one of them it was going to be.

Charles had sensibly requested a formal bill of sale even though, as it appeared, one was not strictly necessary since the cruiser was neither Part 1 registered, nor about to be. In the bill of sale the seller specifically covenanted with Charles that he had the right to sell the boat and that it was free from 'encumbrances'.

In fact, the Sale of Goods Act 1979 would automatically have implied this term into the contract unless there was a clear statement to the contrary. The seller's breach of that term gave Charles the right to demand his money back and claim damage for any other losses he may have suffered as a result – but of course he had to find the seller first and neither Charles nor EFC wanted that trouble or expense.

Unfortunately for Charles, the loser turned out to be him. As we have already seen, a basic maxim of the English law of contract is that you cannot give what you do not have. All that the seller was entitled to transfer to Charles was ownership of 64 mortgaged shares in the boat. Generally, the law does not allow the transfer of encumbrances along with goods, which protects the rights of someone who buys in good faith without being told of the encumbrance; but where a 'legal charge' (or mortgage) of land, an aircraft or a ship is concerned, the position is somewhat different.

In the case of ships (technically, all vessels 'used in navigation not propelled by oars') the Merchant Shipping Act provides that the rights of a mortgagor whose mortgage has been registered under the Act will have priority over all other claimants. A case in 1852 confirmed this principle as applying to future purchasers, even if they had no knowledge of the encumbrance.

So, as Charles's subsequent investigations confirmed, a mortgage had indeed been registered against his boat and was binding on him even though he had been completely unaware of, and unable to discover, its existence. The vessel's entry on the Small Ships Register is a perfectly usual alternative to Part 1 registration, and gave Charles no cause for concern. He had even taken that additional precaution of checking that there was no Part 1 registration. So what else could he have done?

What he in fact undertook was a somewhat cursory investigation of the seller's title, placing too much reliance on the boat's entry in the Small Ships Register. The main purpose of the Small Ships Register is to provide British pleasure-craft owners with a much less cumbersome means of obtaining the documentation necessary to visit foreign waters. It is by no means equivalent to Part 1 registration, and more closely resembles the car log books issued by the DVLC, which record only a vehicle's keeper.

Part 1 registration, on the other hand, does provide evidence of title: the Registrar will have to be satisfied that the title has been traced right back in an unbroken chain to the original builder's certificate. It is also the only means of registering a marine mortgage.

Had Charles investigated title more thoroughly by tracing the vessel's history right back to the builder's certificate, in the same way as the Registrar of British Ships does (and, incidentally, in the same way as title to land is investigated), his suspicions would almost certainly have been aroused at an earlier stage. The seller would have been unable to produce all the prior documentation, since most of it would have been retained by the Registrar. Charles might then have decided to investigate further, abandon the purchase altogether, or perhaps tried to find some insurance cover against any defect in title: a safeguard common in land transactions.

Ironically, had Charles secured his own loan against the boat instead of his house, his own mortgagors would have insisted on registration under Part 1 and on the seller handing over all the previous documentation before paying up. The whole sorry mess might then have been avoided.

The verdict

Charles could have lost £25,000 on this deal. However, by an extraordinary chain of coincidences, his surveyor managed to trace the seller to Spain, where he was living on another boat. The next time this gentleman returned to the UK the police were waiting for him. He was arrested, charged with obtaining pecuniary advantage by deception, tried and convicted. It was not his first such escapade, and he was given the maximum sentence of five years.

The court attached a charge on the convicted man's boat in Spain, which was then sold. This enabled Charles to recover the £25,000 plus interest necessary to pay off the mortgage on *Geraldine X*/*Paragon*.

Case **16 Buyer beware**

The facts

Philip found a second-hand boat for sale on a dealer's forecourt, a 28 ft sports cruiser that seemed something of a bargain at £35,000. The dealer explained that he had taken the boat in part-exchange for a new model, and had marked it down for a quick sale.

The cruiser looked in good condition, and two of Philip's friends who had bought boats from the same dealer said they had no complaints – either about their acquisitions or about his service.

Philip was impressed when the dealer volunteered a distinctly unfavourable survey report commissioned by another prospective buyer less than a month before. The dealer made no bones about the previous buyer having pulled out because of the poor survey, but he took the trouble to go through the report item by item with Philip as they looked over the boat. All the defects listed by the surveyor had been remedied by the dealer's staff, with the exception of a couple too trivial to deter Philip. He bought the boat.

Within a month, he wished he hadn't. The boat's performance was well below his expectations, and on a long offshore passage one engine failed in distinctly uncomfortable weather. It took Philip four hours to limp back into port on one engine, where he called in a local engineer to diagnose the problem.

The engineer's report was sombre. 'A service has been carried out recently', he said, 'but both engines show a history of neglect. It seems possible that, the recent service apart, neither unit has ever been winterised or serviced.' He said that Philip was extremely lucky the remaining one had not packed up on the way back to land. In his opinion, the only solution was to rebuild the whole power installation.

Philip was aghast. Rebuilding would cost a minimum of £6,000, probably more. He had borrowed £30,000 against the security of his house to buy the boat, and with the engines in their current state it wasn't even worth that. He went straight to the dealer and asked for his money back.

The dealer was polite but refused, saying that as far as he was concerned Philip had bought the boat as seen. Philip threatened to invoke the Sale of Goods Act, claiming that the boat was not of merchantable quality. 'But I didn't sell you the boat,' said the dealer. 'I just acted as a broker.' This was news to Philip.

What the law says

It has been explained earlier in the book that the rights of a buyer under the Sale of Goods Act 1979 to return unsatisfactory goods are limited to sales made in the course of business. Sales between two private individuals are therefore excluded. We have also explained that sales through a broker are treated as private sales because the broker acts only as an intermediary.

Ironically, Philip was vaguely aware of this limitation, which is why he had chosen to buy a boat from a dealer. What he didn't know, unfortunately, was that not all dealers actually buy the boats they take in part exchange: some will undertake to sell the craft for a predetermined price, credit the customer's account with the agreed figure, and pay or pocket any difference between that and the eventual selling price. This permits them to retain the status of intermediary, and consequently escape any liability under the Sale of Goods Act.

The dealer is not allowed to conceal the circumstances of the sale, but neither is he obliged to advertise them. The contract between buyer and seller will, of course, show the purchaser who really owns the boat. But many buyers, like Philip, will assume this is just a technical requirement and fail to recognise its significance.

What about the surveyor on whose judgement Philip had relied? To put it at its simplest, a negligent surveyor can be successfully sued for damages, but only by his client – the man who commissions him and pays his fee. He has no liability towards anyone else who may come across the survey and rely on it to his cost, as Philip did.

Philip therefore had no comeback on the surveyor, nor on the vendor, since in a private sale the *caveat emptor* principle applies: it is up to the buyer to beware. He had no comeback on the dealer, because of the dealer's intermediary status. Sadly, there was no peg on which he could hang a legitimate claim.

The verdict

The only thing Philip had going for him was the dealer's concern for his reputation, and the fact that the dealer had agreed a part exchange price of £30,000 with the previous owner. This meant that on the sale price of £35,000, the dealer had made a profit of £5,000 before expenses.

He had also made a profit on the boat he had sold to the previous owner. Despite his overheads, therefore, he had come out of the deal rather better off than Philip, and it wasn't too difficult to persuade him that the best way of protecting his reputation was to forgo some of the profit, so that he was effectively splitting the cost with Philip of the reconditioning. So Philip, while not delirious with the result, had at least managed to halve his losses.

The real point is that Philip should have commissioned his own survey. It is worth reiterating that when a prospective buyer instructs a surveyor, he is not just buying a handful of typed pages at around £50 per page. He also establishes a relationship with the surveyor that puts the surveyor under a legal obligation to him. And if there is negligence, it will be the surveyor – or more likely the surveyor's indemnity insurance – who will pay.

Case **17 Insured peril or fraud?**

The facts

Gavin, an engineer, had been made redundant and was unable to find another job. In better times, he and his wife Jane had owned a small boat and were enthusiastic mariners. So, like hundreds of young couples before them who have found themselves in a similar predicament, they decided to head for the Mediterranean to set up a charter business.

They sold their house in Kent and with the proceeds and the rest of Gavin's redundancy money they bought a 65 ft American-built sports-fisherman in the South of France. Moving on board, they registered the boat with a charter agent and within a week or so they were in business.

Bookings went well for a couple of years, but then began to tail off. Gavin had arranged a small overdraft with a local bank, secured against the boat, to provide a buffer against running and maintenance costs, but as the overdraft mounted the bank became increasingly nervous. Finally they pulled the plug, demanding that Gavin and Jane pay up or sell up.

The couple put the boat up for sale and returned to England, where Jane went back to her old job as a physiotherapist. The boat attracted interest, but no buyers. Several months later, Gavin got a call from the South of France. His boat had sunk at her moorings. He flew out to supervise the recovery and check on the damage.

Once the boat was ashore, it became clear that she had been burgled, vandalised and deliberately sunk. The port engine raw water intake had been disconnected and the seacock opened. The damage was considerable and the boatyard's estimate for repairs

exceeded the price the broker had been asking for the boat: in effect, she was a write-off. Gavin returned to England and lodged a claim with his insurers for the full value of the boat, plus recovery costs.

The insurers appointed a loss adjuster to look into the claim. The loss adjuster took a statement from Gavin and then began to investigate the circumstances. It didn't take him long to establish the recent trading history of the charter business, to find out that the bank were chasing the couple for their money, and to confirm that the boat had stuck on the market. He reported back to his clients.

Weeks went by and Gavin heard nothing from the insurance company. Eventually he contacted them and a couple of days later received a letter making it clear that they had drawn their own conclusions from the loss adjuster's report. The letter baldly stated that the underwriters were not satisfied with the validity of the claim, and that if Gavin wished to pursue it he could do so in court. Gavin asked us for advice.

What the law says

The insurers' reaction was understandable. Even Gavin had to admit that the circumstances suggested a fraud. He had been in the UK when the boat had gone down, but it would not have been difficult for him to recruit someone on the Cote d'Azur to vandalise and sink the vessel for a small fee. Add to that the fact that the sinking could not have been more timely – the bank were now threatening to sue Gavin and his wife – and the case for fraud became pretty convincing.

Most marine policies will cover the policyholder against certain standard risks, which will include 'perils of the sea' and theft and wilful damage caused by someone outside the policyholder's family. Although the wording of marine policies may seem baffling to the uninitiated, there is a reason for the sometimes arcane terminology. The use of phrases and clauses that have already been interpreted and tested in Parliament and the courts precludes further argument about their meaning, and over the centuries Britain's island heritage has provided plenty of opportunity for fine tuning. The result is a tried and tested body of clauses, most of which now have an accepted and, for the most part, sensible meaning.

Take the phrase 'perils of the sea', for instance. It could mean almost anything, but for most people it conjures up pictures of the Beaufort scale, freak waves or whales. What it has actually been held to mean is both more general and more specific: 'every accidental circumstance not the result of ordinary wear and tear, delay or act of the assured, happening in the course of navigation and causing loss to the subject matter of the insurance'.

Tests such as these are not applied inflexibly. Common sense is the order of the day when the courts are attempting to decide what, for practical purposes, was the most direct cause of the loss.

There are, of course, any number of let outs for insurers, particularly where the policyholder can be implicated in the loss – by deliberate conduct, or merely by negligence in the care and maintenance of the vessel.

To return to Gavin and Jane, the insurers had rejected Gavin's claim on the grounds that in their view the loss had been caused not by an insured peril, but by his own deliberate act. Gavin and Jane denied that they were at fault. So far as they were concerned, they had a contract with their insurers, and the insurers were reneging on their obligations. The young couple therefore wanted to enforce the contract.

In such circumstances, a well established principle states that it is up to the assured (ie the beneficiary under a policy) to prove that 'on the balance of probabilities' the loss was caused by an insured peril. It can be difficult to find and produce convincing evidence of what caused the damage, particularly where the vessel has been left unattended for some time. In this respect, Gavin and Jane were lucky. The vandals had forced several locks to gain entry to the boat – an important consideration in dealing with a claim for theft or wilful negligence – and the locks were there to prove it.

In contrast, the insurance company had not succeeded in finding any direct evidence to link Gavin and Jane with the break in. All they had to go on was the circumstantial evidence of the couple's financial crisis: the rest was nothing but speculation.

If the matter went to court, as the insurers knew, the evidence would be tested by the court. Since a Court of Appeal case in 1922, it has been the court's duty, if an assured produces evidence of loss from an insured peril and underwriters offer an alternative explanation, to look at the weight of evidence in support of each alternative. This will enable the court to determine – again, 'on the balance of probabilities' – the cause to which the loss is attributable.

The court should not be deterred from finding in favour of the stronger probability by the fact that some remote possibility exists of the other party's explanation being the correct one. But if, after looking at the evidence, the court is left in doubt as to the cause of the loss, then the assured will have failed to prove his case and will recover nothing.

Here, the insurers were fully aware that Gavin and Jane had firm evidence of the cause of the loss that they were not in a position to challenge. They could produce a motive for Gavin and Jane being responsible for the sinking, but had so far been unable to find any actual evidence linking them with it. They decided to stall for time and call the couple's bluff.

The outcome

Without any money, and living off Jane's earnings, Gavin was in no position to take the insurance company to court, a fact that hadn't escaped the underwriters. The couple's only hope lay in getting legal aid which, being designed for the truly impoverished, is not really a possibility for most boat owners. But the boat had been Gavin's and Jane's home, and their financial plight was now so acute that we felt they might be eligible.

We referred Gavin to a local firm of solicitors who operate the legal aid scheme. The solicitors applied to the Legal Aid Board on his behalf, and in due course we heard that the application had been accepted, giving Gavin the wherewithal to sue the insurance company for breach of contract.

Like so many cases, this one never came to court. The solicitors were required to notify the insurance company that their client had qualified for legal aid. Aware of what they would have to prove to escape their liability, the insurers made a complete about face and paid up on the policy.

In conclusion, it should be said that most good insurance companies do not maintain the cynical approach adopted by Gavin's firm. But all insurance companies have powerful resources and batteries of lawyers at their disposal, in the face of which it can be difficult for policyholders to assert their rights. The only real answer is to avoid giving your custom to firms with a reputation for quibbling over claims. 'Let the buyer beware' is a principle that is just as valid when buying insurance as when buying a boat.

Case **18 It's an ill wind . . .**

The facts

The storm of 1987 brought us a lot of work from insurance companies trying to settle claims in the Chichester and Langstone Harbour area. One of our biggest problems turned out to be actually finding the boats. Scores of them had broken away from swinging moorings and all that could be said was that they were somewhere in West Sussex – but not necessarily in water! One trimaran turned up in a tree in the grounds of a priory – which caused us some interesting difficulties, quite apart from the problem of removing it. Eventually, we had to dismantle the boat and float it away to be reassembled.

A few weeks later, underwriters contacted us to say that they had received a claim from an owner who had lost his 41 ft production motor cruiser. Would we investigate?

We established that the boat, and another identical one moored close by, had both come adrift from swinging moorings and disappeared – although not quite without trace. Wreckage was found on a beach outside the harbour, but we couldn't say for certain which boat it came from.

I went to see the owner of the insured craft, who produced his Certificate of British Registry, photographs of the missing boat and a signed statement saying that the boat had been at her usual moorings immediately prior to the storm. Armed with this information, I contacted the British Registrar of Ships to find out whether there was any marine mortgage outstanding and to check that the policyholder was the registered owner. There wasn't, and he was. So the claim seemed valid, and yet somehow . . .

I can't say why, but my gut feeling was that this was far too neat and tidy. A boat owner truly overtaken by circumstances doesn't take in all the details, with the result that most genuine claims have holes you could drive a 41 ft motor cruiser through. This one didn't.

I decided to dig a little further. The harbour authorities confirmed that the owner had a mooring where he said it was, but couldn't say whether the boat had been at her mooring immediately before the storm.

The Small Ships Register had no record of the boat – not surprisingly, since she was registered as a British Ship. But there was a note against the entry for a similar craft, saying that she had now been sold to a French buyer in Le Havre. The RYA wouldn't release the name and address of the owner, but the date of the sale – just before the storm – rang warning bells.

I went to Le Havre where I found the boat in the marina. Renamed by her new owner, her topsides and flybridge showed no traces of an earlier name, but she bore sufficient resemblance to the lost boat in the photographs to reinforce my feeling that the claim was false. Maybe the storm had come so soon after the sale that the policyholder felt that this was too good an opportunity to miss.

On reading my report, the insurers suggested that I have another talk with the policyholder. As I laid out the facts, his initial indignation crumbled. And when I pointed out the possible consequences of a fraudulent insurance claim, he uttered a few expletives and left. A few days later, the underwriters reported that he had withdrawn his claim.

What the law says

This case raised a couple of interesting legal points. First and foremost, an insurance policy is valid only if the policyholder has an insurable interest in the vessel. The purpose of insurance is to protect policyholders from the financial consequences of an event. For example, an expectant father can insure against his wife giving birth to twins, but he cannot insure against someone else's wife having twins.

Back to boats, though. Obviously an owner has an insurable interest, as indeed might a trustee, a mortgage or loan holder, or a long-term charterer. In some cases, it may not be immediately obvious that an insurable interest is absent. For example, when a yacht is sold and delivery to her new home port is part of the contract, the buyer and seller must agree in advance who is going to be responsible for the insurance and word the contract accordingly. If they do not, the law will make certain assumptions that may not necessarily reflect their original intentions.

What may happen if you don't sort this out in advance is illustrated by the 1932 case of *Piper* v. *Royal Exchange Assurance*. Piper bought the 49 ft yacht *Atalanta II* in Norway and arranged for her to be delivered to Essex. Both the buyer and seller believed that the yacht was the property of the buyer from the moment she left Norway. Piper, therefore, arranged insurance with the Royal Exchange and, when the yacht was damaged en route, he put in a claim.

The insurers refused to pay. In the subsequent court case they were able to prove that, under the contract of sale, legal ownership of the yacht was not transferred to the buyer until she had arrived safely in Essex. Piper thus had no insurable interest in the yacht during the voyage; the court held that the damage was the seller's loss, so the buyer's insurers had no liability to pay out on his claim.

As far as the validity of the claim is concerned, if a boat is lost or damaged and the claim comes to court, it will be up to the insured to prove not only that the damage occurred, but also that the cause of the loss falls within the terms of the insurance policy. It is not enough to point out the simple fact that the vessel is missing, lost or damaged; it is usually important to show that one of the insured perils referred to in the policy document was either the sole cause, or at least a contributory cause, of the loss.

So in the present case the underwriters would have a good defence to any claim by the policyholder, on the grounds of lack of insurable interest and lack of evidence of an insured loss. In addition, if they could prove fraud they would be entitled to reject the claim under a basic rule of contract law that allows the victim of a fraud or attempted fraud to treat the contract as voidable.

Fraud is of course a criminal offence and can be defined as 'obtaining or attempting to obtain property by deception contrary to Section 15 of the Theft Act 1968'. However, because it is a crime, a successful prosecution requires a much higher standard of proof than a civil suit. In a civil suit, one side needs only to prove his case on the balance of probabilities; in a criminal trial, the prosecution has to establish proof beyond all reasonable doubt. In this case, to secure a conviction the court would need to be satisfied that the false statement was made 'knowingly and with a complete absence of belief in the truth'.

It is therefore considerably more difficult for the insurers to prove fraud than to defend their rejection of a claim in a civil suit. Not only that, but an unsuccessful prosecution might mean the policyholder subsequently suing them – for example, on the grounds that their allegations had been libellous.

Finally, even in a seemingly clear cut case such as this, the police would only take the case to court as a criminal prosecution if they were reasonably sure of securing a conviction. A trickster who has covered his tracks carefully will often be able to raise enough doubt in the minds of a jury to ensure that he is acquitted.

With all these considerations, most underwriters will think hard before involving the police. If there are grounds for a charge of fraud, there are probably grounds for rejection; so they might wonder whether it is sensible to take further time and trouble helping the police build a case. Would a successful conviction, assuming they can get one, really bring them any material benefit?

The verdict

After the abrupt departure of the policyholder and the withdrawal of his claim, the insurers were disinclined to pursue the matter. Prosecution, while possibly deterring other would-be fraudsters, would have cost them time and money and, since they never paid out on the claim, they hadn't really lost out. Thus the matter never came to court.

Case **19 A tangle in Portugal**

The facts

A couple of years ago a professional delivery skipper was taking a brand new motor yacht from the UK to southern Spain. Late at night, in heavy weather, the boat was heading south down the Portuguese coast about 7 miles offshore. Suddenly, both engines stopped.

The crew looked over the stern and saw a string of tiny fishing floats decorating the heavy swell. As if on cue, the horizon suddenly lit up with a battery of powerful floodlights. It was apparent the yacht had stumbled into the middle of a vast unlit fishing fleet.

Soon after, a heavy fishing boat hove into view. As she approached, her skipper left the wheelhouse and came forward into the beam of a decklight. Speaking quite good English – at least, a lot better than the delivery skipper's Portuguese – he made it clear to the yacht's crew that they should not attempt to unfoul themselves until dawn.

With the yacht rolling helplessly in the swell, it was an uncomfortable night. At dawn the fishermen began to recover their nets, and the motion changed. It soon became clear to the now very sick crew that the yacht was actually being towed astern by the powerful winch on one of the fishing boats. As the winch dragged them inexorably closer to the boat, the delivery skipper became increasingly worried about the safety of his vessel and crew. He grabbed a large bread knife and tried to sever the tow line of a fishing net as it rose out of the water.

Suddenly, there was a horrendous crash on the other side of the yacht and two well booted fishermen leapt aboard with a proper tow rope which they secured to the winch of the yacht. The yacht's crew had no time to warn them that the line had been led over the bow rail and, as the fishing boat took up the slack, the rail splintered and the starboard quarter of the yacht swung in to collide heavily with the fishing boat.

The damage to the fishing boat was negligible, but the damage to the yacht was severe. Her gunwale had been stove in, and her glassfibre hull was split almost to the waterline. The delivery skipper asked the fisherman to stop while he taped polythene over the hole, but the fisherman's only response seemed to be to increase speed. The skipper tried to make his way forward to cut the tow rope, but the two fishermen still on his deck made it clear that they weren't going to allow him to do so. There was nothing the delivery crew could do but watch helplessly as the water level rose, and hope that they would reach land before the boat sank.

Finally, they made it into harbour, where the fishing boat beached the semi-submerged yacht, causing further extensive damage to the stern gear. The yacht was patched, refloated and lifted ashore. The delivery skipper called his client, the owner of the boat, and was told to take local legal advice.

Before he could do so, the police arrived – but they weren't coming to offer help. The fishermen had lodged an official complaint and, to their horror, the skipper and his crew found themselves under arrest.

The Portuguese Fishing Co-operative levied a claim against the delivery skipper and the owner of the boat for £60,000 worth of damage to nets and catch. The authorities impounded the boat and said they would only release the skipper from prison when the damage claim had been met in full.

What the law says

International maritime law, and relations generally between all the seagoing nations of the world, is closely monitored and controlled by the International Maritime Organisation (IMO), a UN-sponsored body that represents over 95 per cent of global shipping and boating activity. Portugal and the UK are both members of the IMO.

Among the many dozens of international conventions agreed over the years by IMO members, the convention on the arrest of seagoing ships (Brussels 1952) is the one that strikes most fear into lawyers. Under this convention, not only is a member state entitled to detain any ship within its jurisdiction (out to the 12 mile limit), but also any other vessel under the same ownership.

This right is absolute, but it does not allow the authorities to lock you up and throw away the key. Article 5 of the Brussels Convention requires the authorities to release the ship on payment of sufficient bail or security.

In most cases, UK insurance companies will be prepared to act promptly to deal with such emergencies. The standard Lloyd's insurance terms, and the terms of most other marine policies, cover this sort of expenditure under the third party liability section. This states that the underwriters will 'indemnify the assured for any sum which he is legally liable to pay by reason of his interest in the vessel': in the event of the vessel or her crew being arrested, the liability will include putting up sufficient bail or security to ensure their release.

The third party section also covers the cost of all legal representation involved in disputing a collision claim, and any proceedings in Portugal should be paid for by the insurers.

In overseas collisions, your innocence may triumph when the case ultimately comes to court, but it is not necessarily a valid defence on the dockside, especially if it turns out that the local chief of police is the brother-in-law (or whatever) of the skipper of the offending yacht/fishing boat.

In such cases, a yacht can be impounded without much regard for the legal process, and it can be weeks before the yacht is released – particularly if the owner does not have the strength of a renowned insurance company behind him. It is sensible to check the small print before setting out, especially as far as the area of cover is concerned. A case we came across recently involved a collision and arrest in the Aegean off Kos, near the Turkish coast. To his alarm, the skipper discovered that he was not covered by his policy, which limited cover to 'the Mediterranean, not east of 25° E': a restriction that many policies include to prevent their holders straying too near to the powder keg of the Middle East.

Since January 1986 Portugal has been a fully paid up member of the European Community, and incidents of this sort should become less frequent. The Court of Justice of the European Community has a brief to ensure that all member states comply with Community law; this obligation includes 'respect both for the general principles of law and for fundamental human rights'. Human rights include our entitlement to freedom from imprisonment without trial or without good evidence of a criminal offence having been committed. In theory, the victims of this incident would be entitled to take proceedings in the Luxembourg Court; unfortunately, in practice, the procedure is so drawn out that it is unlikely to be of immediate use in the circumstances.

As far as the snagging of the nets is concerned, the ensuing wrangle could keep the Portuguese courts and lawyers busy for months. If all the fishing vessels were unlit, and the court accepted that all the damage had been caused without any negligence or direct action on the part of the delivery skipper, there is no doubt that they would have found in his favour. It is a feature of marine law, however, that a court will rarely find any case to be black and white, and so proportional judgements – where both parties take some of the blame, and therefore some of the liability – tend to be the norm.

In general, when dealing with difficult authorities in the less frequented overseas countries, patience and good temper are more important than simply being in the right – particularly if the yacht has a good supply of duty free stores aboard.

The verdict

Eventually the yacht owner's insurance company agreed to put up bail so that the skipper could be released. However, they weren't prepared to settle the claim, so the delivery crew took matters into their own hands. Leaving their passports in police hands, they jumped aboard a yacht heading south and returned home via Gibraltar.

Negotiations went on for a year. Finally, the Fishing Co-operative's insurance company agreed to meet two thirds of the costs of repairing the yacht, while the yacht owner's insurers agreed to pay for the damaged nets and a small proportion of the damage to the yacht.

The owner ended up with a small loss, which he chalked up to experience, and a year's loss of boating, which upset him rather more.

Needless to say, the delivery skipper hasn't been back to Portugal since, and now always gives it a very wide berth on his way south.

Case **20 Who is responsible?**

The facts

This is probably the most frequent question posed to the courts of the UK, and fortunes have been lost and won as a result of a court's verdict.

John was made redundant at the age of 50, and the employment prospects left open to him were somewhat limited. With the agreement of his wife, he decided to buy an unconverted timber North Sea trawler of approximately 70 ft in length. Many hours were spent with considerable tender loving care in converting the vessel to yacht standards. It was John's intention to take the vessel to the west coast of Scotland and offer her for charter around the islands.

John had seriously underestimated the cost of the conversion and it wasn't long before he started receiving nasty letters from his bank manager. These letters soon became rather more formal and within a few months poor John had been declared bankrupt. His trawler was moved from the marina to a commercial dock where berthing charges were far less.

As a result of John's financial problems, he was unable to pay his insurance premium and the bank was not prepared to assist in any way. A few weeks after the vessel had been delivered to the dock, the dock authorities rang John to say that his vessel had sunk and would he please arrange to remove it immediately.

John managed to get a friend to drive him to the dock and, while he was looking at the part of the superstructure that was still above the water, he seriously considered taking a jump off the nearest pier head. Just at that moment he was approached by someone called Sid. 'Is this your boat?' he asked; John replied that it was. Sid then said, 'I've watched you working on this boat for months in the marina and I was wondering whether you are interested in selling it "as is where is"?'

John could not believe his luck, especially when a figure of £25,000 was suggested. Although no sum was finally agreed, John returned home a much happier man as he knew this amount would lift him out of his financial predicament.

Sid went along to the dock authorities and told them that he now owned the vessel and that he wanted to remove it from the dock floor. The dock authorities offered to hire Sid a heavy-lift crane and, with the assistance of divers, strops were put around the vessel and the lift started. When the vessel was approximately two-thirds clear of the water, there was a loud crack, the vessel broke in half, and then fell back to the dock floor. Sid took off, never to be seen again.

After certain enquiries, it was discovered that Sid had approached a local salvage firm to undertake the task of raising the vessel. Unfortunately, they were so busy that they were unable to assist. However, they informed Sid that it would probably be more beneficial for him to salvage the vessel and claim salvage. Sid's mind went to work and, as no money had been paid to John for the vessel, Sid felt that he could justifiably deduct the salvage costs from the price he had agreed to pay for the vessel.

The dock authorities contacted poor John again to inform him that they had removed the wreckage from the dock floor and that the remains were on the dockside. John went to inspect and on arrival he saw a pile of ash, metal fittings and the engine. To add insult to injury, John was also presented with a bill from the dock authorities for the initial crane hire, plus the costs of the removal of the two halves of the vessel from the dock floor.

John complained bitterly, as he had given no instructions to anybody to recover the vessel – least of all to destroy it and burn it. The dock authorities referred him to their contract, in which it was stated that the liability of removing wreck was down to the owner, and should the owner fail in this undertaking the authority would remove the wreck at the owner's expense.

What the law says

Although it is clear that there was no formal written agreement between John and Sid, a binding contract for the sale of a vessel, of whatever size, can be formed simply in the course of a conversation such as that on the dockside. Unlike an agreement for the sale of land (and that includes buildings permanently attached to the land), which by law must be in writing, even a simple verbal agreement is of immediate legal binding effect. Although it always makes sense to get it in writing, as one party to the contract may start to have second thoughts and time plays tricks with the memory, if both parties acknowledge that an agreement has been made then they are both obliged to carry it through.

In the present case, it would have been better for John to have firmly accepted an offer there and then. Leaving the final figure for later discussion could be enough to prevent a legally binding contract arising, unless they had agreed some firm criteria or formulae for fixing the price at a later stage, in which case it could be said that the price had in fact been agreed.

Another way of reading the situation would be to look at Sid's later behaviour; did he in fact take steps to indicate that he was the owner? His visit to the dock authorities claiming ownership could be his undoing and his statement to the harbourmaster is probably exactly the evidence that John would need to persuade the court that a binding contract had been formed (providing the price or a price formula had been agreed).

But forming a contract, and actually passing the ownership of the property, are two entirely different matters. If indeed a contract was formed on the dockside, when (if ever) did the hull on the dock floor stop being John's property and become Sid's? Sections 17 and 18 of the Sale of Goods Act 1979 lay down the rules for determining when the property in goods passes from seller to buyer in those cases where there is nothing said expressly in the contract itself. Rule I simply states 'where there is an unconditional contract for the sale of specific goods in a deliverable state, the property in the goods passes when the contract is made, and it is immaterial whether the time of payment or the time of delivery, or both, be postponed'. The words 'in a deliverable state' must be interpreted in the light of all the circumstances; John and Sid were talking about a sunken hull on the sea bed and, for the purposes of this contract, and at the price negotiated, there is no doubt that it was in a deliverable state.

Therefore the vessel would have become Sid's property at the time of the contract. It follows that any damage following his becoming owner of the vessel was at his risk, and John would have a valid legal claim for payment of the full contract price, despite the sorry end to the story.

Even if Sid were able to deny the existence of a contract and to convince the court that what had been said on the dockside was no more than an expression of interest, particularly since no price had been agreed, he would still have some trouble in justifying his later action.

Salvage of vessels in danger is a legal concept that goes back to medieval times, and courts have always been prepared to make generous salvage awards to encourage would-be salvors to take the necessary risks to save property in peril. In the present case, however, even if the salvage effort had been successful, and even assuming that Sid had managed to deny the purchase contract, it is doubtful whether he would be entitled to much of a salvage award. The vessel itself was probably in no danger; any damage that could have been done had already been done, and the difference in value between her lying intact on the dock floor or lying intact but water-damaged on the dockside, was probably no more than the cost of hiring the lifting tackle and paying the fees of a salvage engineer.

A further problem that Sid would have faced is whether a salvage claim can be made at all inside a locked harbour. Traditionally, salvage claims could only succeed in tidal waters and, although the Merchant Shipping Act 1988 has extended the definition of tidal waters to include harbours and docks, some question still hangs over the exact status of a dock behind a pair of lock gates; thus a salvage claim might be successfully opposed on this definition.

Having said all that, of course, the operation seems to have gone disastrously wrong; Sid's negligence, or the negligence of his sub-agents, resulted in a perfectly sound (albeit water-damaged) vessel being destroyed. A claim by John against Sid claiming breach of contract for non-payment of goods, with an alternative claim for negligence in interfering with and damaging the vessel, with the salvage contractors named as second defendants to the alternative claim, should get things moving in the courts.

As far as the dock authorities' claim for crane hire and wreck removal expenses is concerned, they should issue proceedings against John, who will apply to the court for the actions to be heard together.

Case 21 VAT trap

The facts

While on a flotilla holiday in the Mediterranean, cruising the Balearic Islands in a small sailing yacht, Bob and Alice put into the Port of Ibiza. The weather had been typically Mediterranean, hot, hazy and hardly a breath of wind. The undersized engine had been buzzing for hours and as far as Bob and Alice were concerned their future Mediterranean cruising would be in a decent motor boat. Having finally made port and found the yacht club bar, they started admiring the many classic old craft lining the quayside.

One beauty that caught Alice's eye was a 60 ft Nicholson from the mid-1930s. Gleaming white topsides, dazzling varnished deck-houses and a crisp blue ensign drew them over to her for a chat with the owner. He turned out to be British and told them he was selling up as she was getting too much for him to manage. When he named his price they could not believe their luck and within minutes a deal was struck, subject to survey, with the owner producing his Certificate of British Registry and bill of sale.

Within a week the surveyor had reported and, apart from a few minor defects, gave the boat a clean bill of health. Meanwhile, Bob had checked the register at the Port of Registry and satisfied himself that the owner was properly registered and that there was no mortgage recorded against the yacht. A contract was drawn up, inquiries made of the local Customs that the sale did not convene Spanish law and that no Spanish taxes were due, and within another week Bob gave the banker's draft for the agreed price in return for the Certificate of Registry and bill of sale.

Although their scheme was to keep the yacht in the Mediterranean, they planned to take the yacht back to the Solent for a season or two for a long refit and to show her off to their friends. The voyage took a trouble-free ten days, the old yacht handled and cruised like a dream and, by the time they reached their first British port of call, they were feeling it was all too good to be true.

It was.

When the Customs officers came aboard to inspect the documents Bob showed them the Certificate of Registry, the contract and the bill of sale, both in good order, but when they asked for a copy of the builder's certificate or original VAT invoice, he could not believe his ears. He explained that the boat dated back to the mid-1930s, had always been in British ownership, and VAT didn't apply until 1973. 'Not so,' said the Customs officer. 'You have bought the boat overseas and, as VAT has never been paid on her, your arrival in the UK counts as an import. I'm putting a stop notice on her until you have cleared this VAT demand, which is 15 per cent of the price paid according to your contract.' Bob and Alice were aghast, locked up the yacht, and went to see their solicitor.

What the law says

Purchasing a used yacht without professional guidance, particularly when she is lying overseas, is a minefield for the unwary. Although this couple had carried out some of the more obvious checks, such as commissioning a survey and checking the title register, and in this case it seems they were lucky enough to have been dealing with a bona fide seller, they unfortunately walked right into the VAT trap.

Relief from double taxation on goods imported from the European Community has been provided statutorily in the UK since 1988. VAT leaflet 702/1/88 gives particulars of how buyers of second-hand boats from other EC states can ensure that they will not be required to pay VAT on returning to the UK. The problem for Bob and Alice is that only goods that have already borne tax in a member state can qualify for this relief, and therefore the relief cannot apply to yachts supplied in the UK prior to the introduction of VAT on 1 April 1973, and which have not borne VAT in any member state.

EC VAT law also allows relief for goods returning to the UK where the person re-importing them was the same person who exported them. If Bob and Alice had been properly advised on the transaction (and who would spend £100,000 on anything but a boat, without proper expert advice?), they would have delayed taking ownership of the yacht until they had her back in the UK. This arrangement, which is perfectly valid and legal, would involve their signing on with the seller as a delivery crew, bringing the boat

into the UK still under the old ownership, and subsequently paying the price and receiving the bill of sale dated after the reimportation had taken place.

Alternatively, if the yacht was to be reimported simply for the purpose of a major refit, HM Customs and Excise have a discretion to waive the VAT charge if prior arrangements are made and no private use is to be made of the yacht, apart from sea trials, during her period in the UK.

Unfortunately the buyers had not taken the trouble to seek professional advice on the transaction and the Customs officers appear to have acted properly in imposing the stop notice and serving the VAT demand.

On a general note, it is worth bearing in mind that after 1991 Customs officers in any EC state will be entitled to inspect not only Certificates of Registry, but also original VAT receipts. If a yacht is for sale on the second-hand market without evidence of VAT having been paid sometime in her career, would-be purchasers should tread warily, as a further VAT demand could be made at any time while cruising abroad. So far as pre-1973 yachts are concerned, Brussels officials are still scratching their heads for an answer.

The verdict

Sadly, Bob and Alice had to dig into their pockets to find a further £15,000, although HM Customs agreed to give them six months to raise the money and varied the stop notice to allow them to take the boat up to her Solent mooring.

Case **22 Left high and dry**

The facts

As the proud owner of a 30 ft cruiser for which he had to pay increasingly painful marina fees over the years, Rick was understandably delighted when the local harbourmaster's office wrote to tell him that his name had finally come up for a mid-river mooring at a fraction of the cost. He knew that although he would miss the convenience of stepping out of his car, walking down a pontoon and on to his boat, the £2,000 saving a year in mooring fees would more than justify the extra trouble, and would enable him to buy a first-class dinghy and outboard.

A visit to the local chandlery provided the perfect answer as far as the dinghy was concerned: a brand-new rigid-floored inflatable which, although of obscure eastern European origin, appeared well built and sturdy and was highly recommended by the salesman. Cash flow was a problem at that particular time, so the salesman was asked to arrange a three-year loan with the Easy Finance Company, a reputable finance house for which they held an agency, and within half an hour the documentation had been drawn up.

Rick wandered through the shop in search of an outboard and, after looking at a whole range of new engines, was delighted to find a three-year-old 6 hp in very good condition at a knock-down price. The salesman explained that it had been taken in part exchange against a more powerful version and, although it did not carry any specific guarantees or manufacturer's warranty, appeared to be a 'nice little runner'. Since he was only intending to use it for short trips within the area, Rick felt it was likely to give years of trouble-free service if properly looked after. For the money involved, it wasn't worth taking out a finance deal, and Rick's credit card provided the answer. Two days later, the dinghy and outboard were delivered.

Rick duly moved his cruiser to his river mooring, and found the new lifestyle very agreeable. With his rigid inflatable and reliable engine, the ferrying to and from his mooring was surprisingly easy, and the rest of the family enjoyed the chance to explore remote parts of the river that his cruiser could not reach.

All went well for a few months, until he noticed that the bonding between the fabric and the GRP floor was starting to separate and other seams were opening up. Worse still, when a surveyor friend was asked to give it the once-over, he pronounced it to be a 'load of rubbish' and said it would probably continue to deteriorate at such a pace that it would be useless within a couple of years of normal usage. As if that wasn't bad enough, the engine was starting to play up, refusing to start, vibrating under power, and eventually refusing to go into gear at all.

Ready with his tale of woe, and quite confident that his legal rights would be respected by the chandler from whom he had bought the boat and engine, he borrowed a trailer and took the whole lot back to claim a refund. When he arrived, his heart sank: the shop was empty, the doors were locked, a closing-down sale had taken place weeks before, and a fading note in the window addressed 'to whom it may concern' stated that the company had been put into receivership. A quick phone call to the receiver confirmed his fears: the assets of the company were insufficient to cover even the secured creditors, and Rick would have to take his place in the queue of unsecured creditors. He knew he was unlikely to get even a penny back.

What the law says

Rick's problem is not an unusual one in times of recession, and despite his legal rights under the Sale of Goods Act 1979 they are of no value in the event of the selling company becoming insolvent. In the unlikely event of Rick being able to prove that he had been sold goods in which defects had been deliberately or fraudulently concealed, then the directors or senior management of the company could be personally liable; however, that is highly improbable in this case. Certainly Rick had a valid claim under Section 14 of the Sale of Goods Act, since the goods that were sold in the course of a business were quite clearly not of merchantable quality; this provision applies equally to new and to second-hand goods, although the court will obviously expect cheaper second-hand goods not to perform quite as well, or quite as reliably, as brand-new goods. In this case, it is likely that a claim would have been successful at least in respect of the boat.

Whether Rick would have been entitled to all his money back and to reject the goods is another matter altogether; the Sale of Goods Act does allow this option to a buyer, but recent case law makes it clear that the buyer must take immediate steps, and within a reasonable time of purchase, to notify the seller of his rejection. In this case, where weeks or months have passed and defects have gradually come to light, it is probably too late to reject.

Rick's remedies will lie in damages based either on the cost of full repair to the standard he was entitled to expect or, alternatively, based on the difference in value between the amount he paid and what the goods were actually worth – bearing in mind their latent defects.

Who does he sue, though? Fortunately, all is not lost, as Rick's means of payment involved credit transactions within the meaning of the Consumer Credit Act 1974. Section 75 of the Act provides that if a debtor (ie Rick, in this case) has a claim against a supplier of goods, in any case involving a debtor/creditor/supplier agreement (ie the purchase of the dinghy) or a credit card arrangement (ie the purchase of the engine), then he will have an equal claim against the creditor (Easy Finance Company, and the bank who issued the card) as he does against the supplier.

This statutory right only applies to agreements for credit of up to £15,000, but it does provide a very real benefit in exactly this sort of case where the supplier of faulty goods is unable or unwilling to honour his obligations under the contract.

The verdict

So far as the defects in the boat were concerned, once the Easy Finance Company had seen a copy of the surveyor's report expanding on his original verbal opinion, with a detailed analysis of the exact areas of weakness, use of unsuitable materials and poor workmanship, they agreed a settlement by which 50 per cent of the outstanding balance on the loan agreement was written off. This was probably a fair compromise, as Rick continued to have the boat available for the relatively restricted use for which he originally bought it, although its second-hand value was very much less than the value of an equivalent boat of reputable design and sound construction.

The engine proved to be more of a problem. Although a qualified engineer stripped the engine down and found severe weakness in the gearbox, he could not safely say that the problem had existed at the time of purchase, and that the supplier was therefore liable for providing goods of less than merchantable quality. Had the engine been new (even leaving aside the manufacturer's warranty), then a trouble-free period of at least two or three years could have been reasonably expected. However, the engine was already three years old and had run for some months without a problem, so the bank who issued the credit card (having taken legal advice) initially rejected the claim. Persistence paid off, though, and after protracted correspondence the bank agreed to cover 50 per cent of the cost of repairs to avoid the need for legal action.

Even banks are wary of getting involved with lawyers, and will go to great lengths to avoid the unexpected turn of events that can occur in court.

Case **23 On the rocks**

The facts

As the owner of a brand new Fairline cruiser, Roy wasn't prepared to cut any corners when it came to insuring his pride and joy. Having heard the many stories about the small print traps, or insurance companies that took months to pay out on a claim, he took care to choose an insurer who was certainly not the cheapest in the market, but who was able to provide the most comprehensive cover available. Roy completed the proposal form with the utmost care before sending it to the insurers, and when he received the policy back some days later he checked it carefully for any errors or omissions. He then filed it away safely with the hope that it could remain there undisturbed until renewal 12 months later.

Roy was the senior partner in his accounting firm and, fortunately, was able to take a month's summer holiday. He decided to take the boat to Holland with the help of a couple of friends, and the arrangement was that his wife, children and in-laws would join the boat at Flushing. There, Roy bade farewell to his two trusty crew members and embarked on the family holiday up through the Dutch canals to Amsterdam. The holiday was a great success until his father-in-law was discovered perusing the attractions in Canal Strasa and, after the proverbial slap on the face, the in-laws flew home from Schipol.

Roy was now faced with somewhat of a dilemma, as his father-in-law had proved to be the only able crew member during their canal trip north. Roy considered contacting his two friends again to assist with bringing the boat back to its base at Poole. After certain assurances given by his wife and two children, he decided to bring the boat back with Mum and children as crew. Roy decided to run back through the Dutch canals, left the large lock at Flushing, and then ran down the coast to Ostend, where they spent the night at the Mercator Marina, adjacent to the town centre.

They left early the following morning and cruised down the Belgian and French coasts in perfect weather. By night the family were safely moored in Le Havre and, after a time at the fair and a good meal, they returned to the boat. Roy listened to the last shipping forecast, then decided to take advantage of the favourable conditions. Mooring lines were slipped at 02.15 hours and, within half an hour, Mum and the children were turned in below. Roy had decided on a night passage back across the Channel, and by 08.00 hours they were moored in Swanage Bay eating breakfast. As the forecast was good, with sunny and calm conditions, they decided to go to Lulworth Cove prior to proceeding to their berth at Poole. The forecast for the afternoon was for a fresh onshore wind to come up.

Unfortunately, Roy had missed the forecast and, worst still, had failed to put out enough anchor chain to cope with the rising tide.

After a good lunch, imbibing a certain amount of the duty-free stock, Roy sent the family ashore in the dinghy and retired to the cockpit for a necessary siesta. He did not notice the increase in the wind, nor did he hear the rumble of the anchor as it broke free of the shingle and started dragging towards the shore. He did, however, stir when the outdrives began hitting the rocks, and by the time the whole boat was wallowing in the surf he was fully awake.

Fortunately for him, a fellow boat owner saw his plight, floated a line down to him with a rubber dinghy, and managed to pull him back to a mooring in deep water. Although the outdrives and hull were damaged, the boat was still intact.

Roy, who was not very experienced in this sort of situation, asked the fellow boat owner what he should do. The fellow boat owner suggested that he towed Roy's boat back to Poole on the basis of a 'drink'. Roy contacted the marina on his portable phone and his Fairline was towed into the travel lift dock. Within a short time the boat had been lifted ashore and chocked up ready for repair. Roy filled in a claim form, truthfully explaining how the incident had occurred, and awaited the reply from the insurers permitting the repairs to go ahead.

Unfortunately, the next communication he received was not from his insurers but from their solicitors; it was not an authority for him to go ahead with the repairs, but a letter denying the liability of their clients to pay for any of the damage incurred in the incident. It was stated that the entire incident had arisen solely as a result of Roy's negligence in failing to listen to the weather forecast, failing to lay out enough anchor chain to deal with rising tide, failing to keep

an anchor watch, and failing to keep sufficient crew on the boat to cope with the emergency.

Roy was understandably distraught. He did not deny that he had been careless, but surely if no one was ever careless, and always took the correct precautions for every eventuality, then there wouldn't be any need for *anyone* to have insurance cover?

What the law says

There are circumstances in which an underwriter is entitled to reject a claim by reason of the insured's negligence. Thus in the case of theft of a vessel, if it had been left open in a place to which the public had easy access, the insurers could well reply on the clause included in most policies excluding claims of theft where a 'lack of due diligence' by the owner was a contributory factor. Similarly, if the damage had been caused by the owner deliberately fitting inadequate ground tackle in an attempt to save money, they may be able to avoid a claim. In this case, however, Roy would probably have the law on his side. The interpretation depends not only on a common sense reading of the policy itself, but also on the application of extensive case law (consisting of High Court and Court of Appeal decisions, many going back to the nineteenth century) and the terms of the Marine Insurance Act 1906. Section 55 of the Act provides that, although the insurer is not liable for any loss attributable to the wilful misconduct of the assured, unless the policy otherwise provides, he is liable for any loss caused by the peril of the sea, even if the loss would not have happened but for the misconduct of the master or crew.

In this case Roy would be regarded in law as having been acting as master, rather than as owner in his negligent seamanship. So long as the insurers could not prove that he deliberately and wilfully let the boat run ashore, he would be entitled to recover his loss, because the actual damage was caused by a peril of the sea – namely, stranding or grounding – even though his negligence had been a contributory factor.

The verdict

Following an exchange of correspondence, the insurers' solicitors put the case to a specialist marine insurance barrister for his opinion. On his advice they agreed to pay out the claim in full, and Roy was back on the water in a few weeks with a great deal more respect for weather forecasts and tide tables. When his policy came to be renewed, though, the insurers had their revenge by adding 30 per cent to his annual premium and doubling his damage excess. In the circumstances, one could hardly blame them.

Case **24 Insurance – don't forget it!**

The facts

Colin was a keen boating enthusiast and, being extremely practical and good with his hands, he had fitted out several boats from standard GRP mouldings. His ultimate objective was to purchase a motor vessel suitable for a transatlantic crossing and, as funds were limited, he decided to buy a commercial vessel that could be converted for leisure, environmental and diving activities. Magazines were purchased and brokers contacted but no suitable vessel came to light.

However, while on holiday with his family in Scotland, Colin discovered an ex-Admiralty 78 ft MFV (Motor Fleet Vessel) virtually derelict in Dundee Harbour. As the vessel was open, he went aboard and discovered that the accommodation was being used as a shelter by vagrants. The vessel was precisely what Colin was looking for and, following various enquiries, Colin managed to track down the owner.

After certain negotiations had taken place, the owner agreed to sell the vessel for £10,000. A purchase contract was drawn up, subject to a reasonable structural survey. A well-known firm of surveyors was instructed, and the report indicated that although the vessel had been neglected for several years the hull and engine were sound. The purchase was completed and Colin took three friends to Scotland to prepare the vessel for sea, and then to deliver it to his home port on the east coast where the conversion work would be undertaken. Work then started on servicing the Gardner 8L3 diesel and gearbox. The deckhouse and hatches were made secure, and a radar and VHF radio telephone were installed.

It was after dark when the vessel finally left Dundee, with Colin having experienced certain difficulties with the telegraph controls to the engine room. As a result of all the excitement, Colin had failed to listen to the shipping forecast that was giving NE force 4–5, increasing to NE force 7, possibly gale force 8.

All went well until they cleared St Abbs Head, when the weather deteriorated considerably with an unpleasant port beam sea. The vessel started shipping water and, after approximately one hour, the main engine-driven bilge pump failed. Colin went below to inspect the suction pipe strainer. He lifted a hatch in the sole and discovered that the water had risen to approximately 4 ft above the strainer. Colin stripped off and submerged himself in the bilge water. Soon he discovered that the remains of two rats had been sucked into the strainer. The furry contents were removed, and the bilge level dropped to an acceptable level. Apart from the inclement weather, and considerable discomfort to the crew, the vessel arrived safely at its destination.

Colin engaged the services of a local boatyard to remove the deckhouse and decking and, accompanied by a friend who was a shipwright, started work on the conversion. Several months later, the vessel was unrecognisable. A new deck had been laid and a new deckhouse and bridge had been installed. The boatyard had installed a 25 KVA generator, complete with a commercial distribution panel, and serviced and repainted the main engine and gearbox. The vessel was pristine and complemented Colin's technical skills. Sea trials were carried out and the vessel performed admirably.

On Sundays, the boatyard was normally closed. However, the manager gave Colin a key to the main gate so that he could let himself in to work on his vessel. On one particular Sunday morning Colin noticed two likely lads removing equipment from a nearby boat. Colin kept a low profile, but noted the number of their van.

The following day Colin was approached by the yard manager, who mentioned that there had been a number of thefts from boats over the weekend. Colin was interviewed by the local police and gave a statement as to what he saw on the Sunday morning. He later understood from the yard manager that the two lads in question undertook certain subcontracting work around the boatyard for the manager at weekends. Colin became worried about the safety of his own vessel and suggested to the manager that the lads should be banned from the premises.

The following Sunday night Colin received a telephone call from the yard manager who told him that his boat had exploded and that four fire engines were on the scene. Colin rushed to the yard to see his pride and joy engulfed in flames. As he approached, he tripped over the charred remains of a body on the quayside. A policeman asked him if there had been any crew aboard the vessel, to which Colin replied 'No'. He was then asked if he could identify the quayside body. He realised that he could. It was one of the lads he had seen in the yard the previous Sunday morning.

The following morning, a fireman discovered the unrecognisable remains of the other man in the flooded bilges. The police forensic department established that approximately 5 gallons of petrol had been poured down the air conditioning intake. Petrol vapour had then been pumped below decks and a spark, most probably from the air conditioning fan, had detonated the explosive mixture, blowing the vessel apart and killing the two arsonists.

As a result of the conversion of the vessel, Colin had landed himself in considerable debt and had to remortgage his house to cover costs. Regrettably, Colin had overlooked his insurance and his only course of action was to sue the boatyard. Colin instructed his solicitor, and a High Court writ for £125,000 was served on the boatyard. As Colin was the plaintiff, he had to place a substantial amount into court to cover costs, etc. After two days of the hearing, Colin's QC was not optimistic about the outcome; also, costs could well exceed the value of the claim. Colin realised that he was fighting the boatyard's insurance company who, as a matter of principle, were going to defend to the bitter end the action against the boatyard. Colin could not afford to gamble his or his family's future on the eventual outcome of the case and, on advice, he withdrew his action.

What the law says

While a number of complex legal questions arise out of this case, one of the main points at issue was the legal relationship between Colin and the boatyard and the recently deceased 'likely lads'.

To summarise the legal position, when someone is paid to look after another's goods, then the law considers that person to be a bailee of those goods, and accordingly imposes rigorous responsibilities upon him in relation to those goods while they are in his control. Those responsibilities apply irrespective of whether it is a dry cleaners with suits on their premises or, as in this case, a small boatyard having care of a large motor vessel.

While the full scope of a bailee's duties are too broad to consider in this case study, the law says that a boatyard, as bailee, must take reasonable care of the vessel and keep her in a safe place. It states that the boatyard will be liable to the owner for any loss or damage to the vessel caused by the negligence of the boatyard or its employees, including the boatyard's agents or subcontractors, provided that those agents or subcontractors were acting within the scope of their employment when the loss or damage to the vessel was sustained. This duty even extends to making the boatyard liable for the subcontractors' fraud or dishonesty, provided again that the loss or damage arose out of the subcontractors' purported performance of their duties.

In this case, it is clear that the 'likely lads' were subcontractors and it follows that the boatyard could be liable for the actions of the 'likely lads', provided that it could be shown that the damage or loss arose while the 'likely lads' were carrying out their appointed duties. Unfortunately, in this case, Colin would run into considerable difficulty in establishing this, since the boatyard would properly maintain at the trial that the 'likely lads' had never been employed to demonstrate their limited pyrotechnic skills on Colin's boat and that their return to the boatyard with the petrol cans on Sunday evening did not form part of any agreement to work overtime on Colin's vessel.

In these circumstances, Colin would have had to fall back upon an even less tenable legal argument to the effect that the manager's apparent inability to prevent the 'likely lads' from returning to the boatyard that evening, and the consequential destruction of Colin's vessel, in itself represented such a failure to protect the vessel from inherent danger as to amount to an act of negligence on the part of the manager (and consequently also the boatyard).

As has been pointed out in previous case studies, the tort (or civil wrong) of negligence can be compared with the Grand Banks as a fertile fishing ground for legal debate. Many a lawyer has returned from a voyage to those parts with enough gold to buy a vessel of his own. It is an area of the law to be avoided, since few things are certain until a judge says they are, and by the time you get to that point you are likely (as was Colin) to be on a leeshore with limited room to manoeuvre.

In order for Colin to pursue his claim that the boatyard had been negligent in this instant, he would have to prove that a number of specific legal requirements were satisfied.

First, the court would have had to have been satisfied that 'a duty of care' existed between Colin and the boatyard. This can normally be shown to be present by virtue of a relationship of trust between the parties. In this case the court would have accepted that the boatyard owed such a duty to Colin, as the owner of a vessel stored on their premises. The second requirement would be that Colin would have had to have shown that there had been a breach of that duty of care. Typically, this would involve some act of careless behaviour on the boatyard's part.

In deciding whether or not the boatyard had been careless, a court would adopt the standards of a reasonable man. In this case, what is the careless behaviour of the manager that Colin complains of? There is no evidence that the manager continued to employ the 'likely lads' at the boatyard following the earlier incident. Even if they had been so employed, would a reasonable man have considered that the manager's actions in allowing them to carry on working at the boatyard premises, amounted to an act of careless behaviour? This certainly would have been an arguable point.

Unfortunately, Colin's case would have failed at the third fence, as he would have had to have shown to the court that the damages and the loss that he had sustained were a foreseeable consequence of the manager's careless behaviour. It is difficult to see that any court would have accepted this as, on the face of it, the manager had no cause to suspect that the 'likely lads' had any intentions of destroying Colin's vessel by arson. Had they merely stolen items from his vessel, then the situation might have been somewhat different.

In the circumstances, Colin did not have a legal redress against the boatyard, but did he have a claim that could be pursued against any other parties? The 'likely lads' were 'men of straw' and their estates were so small that they were 'not worth the powder and shot' of litigation.

What of the police? Did the fact that the police identified Colin to the 'likely lads' as the principal witness to their light-fingered activities of the previous Sunday give him any course of action against them? The answer is No, because a defendant in criminal proceedings is perfectly entitled to know who is making accusations against him and the police are under no legal duty to withhold the identity of their witnesses – although in normal circumstances, they would not be unnecessarily free with this information.

Had Colin sustained personal injury as a result of the arson attack on the vessel, then he could have made a claim against the Criminal Injuries Compensation Board in respect of those injuries. Unfortunately, the Board only accepts claims from persons who have suffered a physical injury as a result of a crime; and an application by Colin for compensation in respect of his distress and shock at seeing his life savings burning away at the quayside would have been met with a sympathetic but negative response.

The verdict

Colin was regrettably ill advised to have commenced proceedings in this case, or to have maintained them when it became clear that the insurance company was going to defend this action to the bitter end. 'The man in the street' should carefully consider his position before embarking upon litigation of this nature, since it is far too easy to throw 'good money after bad' in so doing.

As it was, the yard manager was not going to make a particularly impressive witness and the insurance company were somewhat concerned at the risk (however slight) of a decision being made by the court that might have had the effect of extending the scope of an employer's legal responsibility for the criminal acts of subcontractors. In the event, the action was withdrawn upon the terms that each party would bear their own legal costs. Colin lost a lot of money, but drew comfort from the fact that he could easily have lost a great deal more if he had not taken the difficult decision to withdraw his claim. He will certainly ensure that any vessel he owns in the future is properly and adequately insured.

Case **25 A question of ownership**

The facts

Lawrence was a young man with a growing family. His 'eldest child' was a Fairey Huntress which he had picked up for a song some ten years ago, before their virtues made them so sought after. Much as he loved the vessel, he had to concede his wife's point that she was a little too small for the family needs and so, reluctantly, he advertised the Huntress for sale in the yachting press. This produced an immediate response, and Lawrence's phone rang almost continuously for the next week.

Alan was the first man lucky enough to make contact. Lawrence described the Huntress to him over the phone and Alan indicated that he was a serious would-be purchaser. Lawrence was a man of principle and, while taking the names and phone numbers of subsequent callers, made it clear to the other would-be purchasers that Alan was 'first in line'. Alan eagerly agreed to Lawrence's suggestion of a trial sail and, a few days later, they met at the marina at Chichester where the Huntress was berthed.

Lawrence showed Alan all around the vessel and then they took her out for a trial run, motoring gently down to Chichester Harbour and out into the clear expanse of Hayling Bay, where Lawrence could show off the Huntress's performance without incurring the wrath of the harbourmaster and the numerous dinghy sailors who were making the best of a fine summer's day.

Alan was very impressed by everything he saw and agreed to buy the vessel there and then without a survey. Alan then explained that he worked abroad and that his money was kept offshore. Furthermore, he told Lawrence that he would be going abroad again shortly and he wanted to tie up all the formalities as quickly as possible. The Huntress was Part 1 Registered, and Lawrence obtained a standard bill of sale in anticipation of the transfer of ownership following the sale. In order to help Alan in concluding the purchase without delay, Lawrence allowed himself to be persuaded to execute a bill of sale in favour of Alan, and handed same to him, together with the Certificate of British Registry and the British Tonnage Certificate that had come with the vessel. Alan and Lawrence agreed that the Huntress would remain Lawrence's property until the purchase monies were received by him the following week.

Seven days came and went, and there was still no sign of Alan's money. Lawrence telephoned Alan and was informed by his mother that he had gone back to Brunei, and the familiar 'cheque in the post' scenario unfolded. After four weeks of repeated phone calls and letters Lawrence's patience finally expired, and he wrote to Alan informing him that he had 28 days in which to pay the purchase money to complete the transaction, failing which Lawrence wanted the ship's papers returned to him, as it was his intention to readvertise the vessel for sale. Alan acknowledged the letter, but did no more.

Fortunately, Lawrence had kept a note of the other interested purchasers and, six weeks later, he was showing Bob over the vessel. Bob was keen to proceed with the purchase, even when Lawrence explained the problem over the ship's papers. After a satisfactory survey, Bob agreed to pay Lawrence's asking price. Bob thereafter handed Lawrence a cheque for 10 per cent of the sale price, which was drawn on the personal account of Samantha. Lawrence noted this fact and asked Bob about the signature on the cheque. Bob assured Lawrence that Samantha was lending him the money to purchase the vessel.

Two days later Bob delivered Lawrence a cheque for the balance of the purchase money. This cheque was also drawn on Samantha's account. Both the cheques were duly cleared and Lawrence gave Bob the keys and such papers as he still had in his possession. A short time later, Bob told Lawrence that he intended to take the Huntress from Chichester to a boatyard in Cowes where he was going to have extensive work undertaken to bring the Huntress up to Concourse standard. Bob told Lawrence that the boatyard had limited space available for storage of the vessel gear and, since he lived in a relatively cramped London flat, he eagerly accepted Lawrence's offer to store the more readily removable items of the vessel's gear, which included most of the more expensive navigational aids and the good-quality semi-rigid tender and outboard. Lawrence and Bob carefully placed the items in Lawrence's garage.

The next day Lawrence received an anguished phone call from Samantha, who maintained that she was the true owner of the Huntress as she had advanced Bob the money to buy the vessel. Samantha told Lawrence that she and Bob had been lovers and that Bob had taken her money and bought the boat shortly before announcing that their affair was at an end. Lawrence listened sympathetically to Samantha's story, but pointed out that the sale had already taken place and that, apart from the gear that he was storing, he had no further control over the matter.

Lawrence immediately got in touch with Bob, who was extremely reticent about the matter but said that he would make contact with Lawrence to collect the vessel's gear in due course.

Two days later Bob and Lawrence were served with a writ issued by Samantha's solicitors, in which it was claimed that Samantha had entered into an agreement with Bob for the purchase of the Huntress whereby Samantha would be the owner of the vessel, but Bob would have the rights to use it. The writ included a claim that

Lawrence would transfer ownership of the vessel to Samantha. Accompanying the writ was a court order directing that Lawrence should not part with any of the items of the ship's gear that were still in his possession until the dispute as to ownership had been resolved.

To make matters worse, Alan reappeared at Lawrence's house two days later with a banker's draft for the original agreed purchase sum demanding that Lawrence proceed to complete the sale of the vessel to him as agreed several months before. When Bob told him that the vessel had been sold, Alan turned rather nasty and produced the ship's papers, which showed that the vessel had been re-registered in Alan's name. Alan then left, stating that he was going to instruct a solicitor as he was going to sue Lawrence for breach of contract, and contest both Bob's and Samantha's claims to ownership of the vessel on the grounds that he was the vessel's registered owner. Lawrence sought legal advice.

What the law says

It is clear that there was a binding contract between Lawrence and Alan for the sale of the vessel. Lawrence even, rather unwisely, completed the bill of sale enabling the vessel to be registered in Alan's name even though Alan hadn't paid the purchase money. Lawrence did, however, sensibly retain possession pending payment of the purchase price and, in doing so, he exercised the unpaid sellers lien under Section 48 of the Sale of Goods Act 1893 (now 1979). The effect of this Act is to enable the unpaid seller to re-offer the goods for sale, having given the purchaser due notice of his intention to do so if the contract is not completed by payment in full being made by a specified and reasonable time.

Lawrence sensibly appreciated that Alan's circumstances were such that he would need to be given a little more notice of Lawrence's intention to resell the vessel elsewhere than would normally be the case. Alan acknowledged receipt of the letter in which Lawrence gave him the appropriate notice and, in the circumstances, Lawrence was perfectly entitled to offer to sell the vessel to someone else.

Far from having a claim against Lawrence for breach of contract, the converse applies in that Lawrence has a claim against Alan for his loss and damages arising out of Alan's breach of the contract regarding payment of the purchase money of the vessel. Lawrence is, however, only entitled to claim for his actual losses arising out of the breach of contract. As he did not have to readvertise the vessel, and he received the full asking price from Bob some two months later, his most obvious claim would be for the two months' extra mooring fees and for the general costs and expenses incurred in contacting Bob and making arrangements for the subsequent resale, and for maintaining the insurance cover on the vessel during the additional period.

What is the effect of Alan being the registered owner of the vessel? Registration is not conclusive proof of title to the vessel, but it does result in a shifting of the burden of proof of ownership. Thus if Lawrence, Bob or Samantha wish to claim ownership, the onus is on them to rebut the legal presumption that Alan is the true owner. Leaving aside the question of whether Alan's actions in applying for reregistration of the vessel was lawful, in the circumstances it is clear that Alan would not be able to maintain his claim to ownership based solely on the registration particulars.

What then of the competing claims of Bob and Samantha to ownership of the vessel? The answer to this revolves around the nature of the relationship between Bob and Samantha and the capacity in which Bob approached Lawrence to negotiate the purchase. The only inkling that Lawrence had of Samantha's involvement was through the signature on the cheques. Bob gave a perfectly adequate explanation for this and Samantha's own admissions that she had lent Bob the money to buy the vessel clearly supports Bob's claims that he was contracting solely on behalf of himself for the purchase of the Huntress. Samantha clearly has a right of action against Bob for recovery of the sums lent, but that in itself does not entitle her to ownership of the vessel. Lawrence has received the purchase money, and Bob has possession of the Huntress.

The contract was accordingly completed, and ownership of the property passed to Bob before Samantha even appeared on the scene. Lawrence therefore cannot transfer ownership of the Huntress to Samantha, as ownership has already passed to Bob.

What then of Bob's and Samantha's competing demands for the release of the items of gear? If it was clearly agreed between Lawrence and Bob that the Huntress was sold with all her gear, then ownership of the gear passed to Bob upon completion of the purchase. Lawrence's subsequent agreement to store the property does not affect this, but in view of the court order he would be well advised to ensure that the items are not passed on to Bob and that they are kept in a safe place until the competing claims are resolved.

The verdict

Alan instructed his solicitors, who explained the full extent of his legal situation to him. He sensibly thought better of becoming further involved and, with the consent of all parties, returned the original ship's papers to Lawrence. All parties took a long, hard look at the situation and Samantha ultimately had to accept that Lawrence had contracted with Bob for the sale of the vessel, and that Bob was therefore entitled to both possession of the Huntress and to be registered as her owner. Bob agreed to allow a marine mortgage to be registered against the vessel on Samantha's behalf, thus protecting her interests while they went on to argue about other matters arising out of their relationship. Lawrence was able to release the gear back to Bob so that his wife could put her car back in the garage.

He will exercise much more caution when both buying and selling vessels in the future and will certainly ensure that no ship's papers are released until all the loose ends have been tied up.

Case **26 Check up on your surveyor**

The facts

At the age of 59, Professor Hobson decided to retire from his university post so that he could fulfil his lifelong ambition to cruise the European canals and write his memoirs. Although keen on boating, the Professor was not very practically minded, and over the years he and his wife had enjoyed the hospitality of their many boat-owning friends. One year, the Professor and his wife had chartered a canal cruiser in France for their annual holiday and, with the assistance of his daughter and her husband, they had enjoyed a very successful holiday.

The Professor called on the help of his friends to advise him on a suitable boat for the passage through Europe. The boat had to be a live-aboard with sufficient accommodation for the occasional friends who would join them during their passage. The boat also had to have a reasonably shallow draft, and low air draft.

The Professor bought all the boating magazines and, with academic meticulousness, listed on his computer every vessel that might be suitable along with the name of the broker or vendor. Soon a list of 17 boats had been formulated and, marking every boat in points out of 100 for its suitability, a shortlist of five was drawn up. All five boats were inspected in the following weeks, with the result that two were of particular interest. Boat number 3 was ideal, although slightly beyond the Professor's modest means. Boat number 2 was also suitable, had sufficient accommodation, but its drawback was the fact that it was built in the early 1960s of double diagonal construction. The broker showed them over the second boat again and, after lengthy discussions, the Professor made an offer subject to survey.

Two days later the broker told the Professor that his offer had been accepted, and could he arrange for the boat to be surveyed as quickly as possible. The Professor asked if the broker knew of any local surveyors, and he was given two names. The boat was duly surveyed and sea-trialled. The report indicated that, in principle, the boat was sound. However, it required certain minor works to bring it up to scratch.

Delighted with this report, the Professor completed the sale and the boat was his. During the following months, various recommendations made in the survey report were undertaken by a local boat-yard, including resealing all windows, portlights and hatches, recaulking the teak laid deck in a number of areas, cleaning off and antifouling the bottom, painting the topsides, cabin sides and coach-roof, and rubbing back and revarnishing all the brightwork. During this period, the Professor and his wife concentrated on the interior. All carpets and soft furnishings were replaced, and every spare area had a book shelf installed. The navigation area was modified to accept a word processor, with the intention of making this the Professor's workplace.

The boat was of a popular design, 38 ft long, built during the early 1960s. The hull construction was double diagonal, cascover sheathed to just above the waterline. The decks were of marine ply overlaid with teak; the cabin sides and coachroof were also constructed from marine ply.

Once all the work was completed, the Professor, aided by various friends, undertook numerous sea trials prior to their departure across the Channel. The boat performed admirably during the sea trials, and in the early spring the Professor, his wife and two trusty boat owner friends left the south coast bound for Le Havre where they would enter the European canal system. Although the previous 24-hour weather forecasts had been listened to and logged with care, no one could have predicted the very serious deterioration in the weather 10 miles off Le Havre.

Within a short time, both the port and the starboard engines had failed. One of the Professor's friends very quickly replaced the filter elements, primed the engines, and soon both were running again. However, after approximately 10 minutes the port engine failed, quickly followed by the starboard. The engine hatches were lifted and, to everyone's horror, the bilge water had risen to a level just above the gearboxes. The engine room bilge pump was immediately turned on, but could only just keep pace with the ingress of water. After replacing the filter elements, the Professor's friend turned off the raw water intake to the starboard engine, disconnected the hose, and strapped it down into the bilge water. Both engines were started and soon the bilge water was down to an acceptable level.

After discussions, they decided to proceed on the port engine towards Le Havre, running the starboard engine only as and when required to reduce the bilge water level. Soon the port engine had failed yet again. The starboard engine was started, but very soon after this engine stopped as well. As sea water was entering the boat at an alarming rate, the Professor decided to put out a mayday.

Within 25 minutes, during which time the conditions had further deteriorated, the Le Havre lifeboat – armed with enormous balloon fenders – came alongside. Immediately two of the lifeboat crew leapt aboard and, within a matter of minutes, the Professor's pride and joy was under tow with a high-capacity diesel pump removing the bilge water. On their arrival in Le Havre, the travel lift was on stand-by and, within no time at all, the vessel was chocked up safely ashore. After numerous forms had been filled in, a very forlorn Professor and his crew checked into a local hotel.

The following day, a full inspection of the hull was undertaken by a local boatyard. The findings were that the seam between the keel and the bottom planking had opened up over the whole length, and that the two main fuel tanks were suffering from bacterial infestation, which in turn blocked the two filters. Certain areas of the cascover sheathing were removed to check the full extent of the damage. The Professor was horrified at the findings. It appeared that, in the areas inspected, there were serious problems of rot.

The Professor was advised to enlist the services of a recognised English surveyor to make a thorough inspection and to advise accordingly. The surveyor's comments in his report stated that, as a result of extensive hull rot beneath the cascover sheathing, the vessel was structurally unsound and should not under any circumstances be used in a seaway until all the double diagonal bottom planking had been replaced. Had the Professor known of the full extent of the defects within this boat, he quite definitely would not have gone ahead with the purchase. Not knowing what to do, he contacted his solicitor in England.

What the law says

Regrettably, the Professor's problem is not as uncommon as is sometimes thought. He has certainly been the party to an extremely unwise purchase, but what are his remedies and against whom?

Had the vendor of the boat been a company or an individual trading in second-hand motor yachts, then the Professor would almost certainly have a right of action against them for recovery of his losses on the grounds that the vendor was in breach of Section 14 of the Sale of Goods Act, which requires that the goods supplied under the contract are of merchantable quality and reasonably fit for the purpose for which they are being bought. Unfortunately, in this instance, the previous owner of the yacht was a private individual and so the Sale of Goods Act did not apply.

What is the position between the Professor and his surveyor? Has the surveyor been negligent? As those of you who have read the earlier case studies will know, in order for the Professor to pursue a claim for negligence against the surveyor he would have to prove that a number of specific requirements were satisfied. First, the Professor would have to prove that a 'duty of care' exists between himself and the surveyor. In this instance, the Professor was clearly placing his trust in the surveyor, so such a duty of care clearly existed. The second requirement is that the Professor would have to show a breach of that trust. In considering whether or not there had been a breach of the trust, the court would have regard to the 'reasonable man test'.

The law expects that any party, holding himself out as having a professional skill, will show the average amount of competence associated with a proper discharge of the duties of that profession. If he (or she) falls short of that, then he or she is not behaving reasonably. In this case, the surveyor was instructed because of the Professor's concerns regarding the age and construction of the vessel. A competent surveyor should have known that the seam between the keel timber and the bottom planking (garboard seam) was a vulnerable part of the vessel's construction, and it is assumed that a proper examination of this seam would have revealed the defect that could so nearly have resulted in a tragedy.

Similarly, the surveyor should have made efforts to ascertain the integrity of the hull underneath the cascover sheathing by using a spike or sounding hammer, or actually stripping off part of the sheathing. However good the sheathing may have appeared, it was inevitable that a certain amount of moisture would have found its way through the sheathing over the years, with the danger that, as in this case, active rot can be concealed by apparently sound sheathing. The surveyor should have had these matters uppermost in his mind when inspecting the vessel. The fact that he did not discover these defects clearly indicates that he was not behaving reasonably in carrying out his professional duties in this instance.

The third ingredient of the tort of negligence is that the Professor's damages and losses have been caused by the surveyor's breach of duty of care and are not too remote a consequence of it. Clearly, the Professor will have sustained substantial losses when the necessary repairs have been completed, which he would not have had if the surveyor had carried out his task properly.

Based on the above advice, the Professor's solicitors wrote to the original surveyor seeking his proposals for compensating the Professor for this loss. Unfortunately, it then became apparent that the surveyor had no professional qualifications whatsoever, having effectively turned his hand to surveying after a lifetime career as an artist. When asked whether he held insurance, the only document that he could produce referred to the contents of his council flat and the third party cover as to his ancient van. The Professor realised that he was in serious difficulties, as the surveyor was a 'man of straw' with no professional indemnity insurance against which the Professor could pursue a claim for his losses.

The Professor's solicitors thereafter contacted the brokers who, it is to be remembered, specifically recommended the services of the surveyor in question (albeit leaving the final choice to the Professor). Did the Professor have a claim for negligence against the brokers for having suggested he use a surveyor who was both incompetent and lacking in means or indemnity insurance?

This is an altogether more complicated matter. Effectively, the Professor would have to show that the brokers owed him a duty of care when advising him as to the choice of surveyor, notwithstanding that they were clearly retained by and acting for the original owners of the yacht throughout the transaction. Certainly, the Professor did not enter into any separate or formal contract with the brokers whereby they agreed to advise him in this matter. It is thus doubtful whether the Professor would have ever been able to establish in court that the brokers owed him 'a duty of care'.

The verdict

Notwithstanding the uncertainty as to the eventual prospects for success, a formal claim was made against the brokers, who sensibly handed the matter over to their indemnity insurers. A short but intense round of negotiations ensued. The insurance company appreciated the weakness of the Professor's claim, but they took the view that they did not wish to incur the avoidable legal costs and cause adverse publicity for their insured. The Professor was equally well advised by his solicitor as to the dangers of pursuing the claim to trial, having regard to the costs of doing so and the limited prospects of a successful outcome.

Ultimately, the insurers agreed to pay one-half of the costs of the repair of the vessel on the basis that the Professor bore the other half and his other losses. All parties were, if not happy with the outcome, equally unhappy, which is sometimes as good as you get!

The Professor has certainly learnt by his experience and will ensure that when instructing a surveyor in the future he ascertains that the surveyor is a member of the appropriate professional body or institution (be it the Royal Institute of Naval Architects, the YDSA, or the Society for Underwater Technology); and, most importantly of all, that the surveyor holds current indemnity insurance in the sum appropriate, not only to the value of the vessel to be surveyed, but also to the extent of any consequent losses that he anticipates he may suffer in the event of the whole transaction proving to be a disaster.

Case **27 Contractor or subcontractor?**

The facts

Ian had spent a lifetime building bridges and roads in the more inhospitable areas of the world and was reaching a stage in life where he was beginning to look forward to a serene retirement in one of the warmer Mediterranean countries. In preparation for this, he began to look for a suitable modestly sized launch so that he could keep himself out from underneath his wife's feet and indulge in that most enjoyable of pastimes: sitting aboard your own boat on a sunny mid-week afternoon, thinking of more unfortunate colleagues who are still having to work for a living!

Ian scrutinised the yachting press at length, albeit belatedly, since it took some time for the magazines to be sent to him in the remote corner of Venezuela where his final contract had taken him. His eye was caught by an advertisement for a suitable vessel.

He contacted the company that described itself as the manufacturer in the advertisement and, after considerable discussions and negotiations over the phone, combined with a fleeting visit to the company's offices while on leave in the UK, he was able to agree upon a firm and extremely competitive price for the supply of the launch, together with various additional extras, including a trailer and an auxiliary outboard.

He had read of the various problems that can arise when a building contract is not formally entered into, and so was happy to enter into the standard BMIF build contract with the company. Of a total purchase price of £20,000, he agreed to pay stage payments of 25 per cent upon the signing of the agreement, 25 per cent upon completion of the hull, 25 per cent upon completion of the interior and installation of the engine, and a final 25 per cent upon completion of the acceptance trial and the signing of the satisfaction note.

In view of the fact that the vessel was to be sent to Spain upon completion, the contract was expressed to be VAT zero rated. Ian sent back the first £5,000 with the signed build agreement, and some time later he received a letter from the company confirming that the hull had been completed and requesting the release of the further £5,000. Being a trusting chap, Ian sent off his money and within a few weeks had received confirmation from the manufacturers that the interior of the vessel had been completed and the engine installed and the penultimate balance of £5,000 was due.

Ian paid the third instalment and, much hampered by the distance and the time difference, began to make arrangements for the vessel to be taken to Spain on a low-loader immediately upon her formal delivery from the company, so as to ensure that she was out of the UK within the seven-day deadline set by HM Customs and Excise with regard to the VAT regulations.

It was at this stage that Ian became aware of the fact that the company who had signed the build agreement as 'the Builder' had not actually undertaken any of the physical building works, but had effectively passed on the whole job to third party subcontractors. To make matters worse, the company had for some time been in financial trouble and, while accepting Ian's £15,000 payments as manna from heaven, had only paid a portion of the monies received to the subcontractors who had not been paid for some four months; notwithstanding this fact, the subcontractors had continued to work on the vessel so that she was virtually complete.

By the time Ian discovered the situation, the subcontractors had seen the writing on the wall and had ceased work on the vessel, chaining it (and a number of other less complete hulls owned by other unfortunate individuals) to the inanimate bulk of a rusted works crane to ensure that the would-be owners did not adopt the well-known legal remedy of 'self help' in resolving their disputes with the company which had, by this time, ceased to answer any correspondence and was actively seeking to go into liquidation.

To make matters worse, while the company had received the additional payments from Ian in respect of the trailer and the auxiliary outboard, it had only sent a proportion of these monies to the respective suppliers, who were now refusing to deliver the items or indeed give Ian credit for the sums that had been paid on the basis that these monies had to be returned to the company's receivers.

Ian was eventually able to contact one of the company directors and the whole unfortunate picture emerged. The company had, probably quite genuinely, quoted its price on the basis of subcontracting losses that had proved to be wildly inaccurate. The company had thus made a loss on each sale and, as a result of pressure from its bank, had been to see its accountants, who had advised the insolvent company that it had to be liquidated.

The company had no assets and substantial preferential creditors. Furthermore, it did not have the means, or indeed the intention, of paying the subcontractors the sums due to them to secure the release of the launch. Ian was invited to join the growing queue of unsecured creditors who had no prospects of seeing their money again.

Ian contacted the subcontractor and, while they were sympathetic to his situation, they were somewhat more concerned about their own since, as a small outfit, they had invested most of their available capital and staked much of their future on the success of their contract with the company. In fact, all that they had to show for this contract was a large debt and a number of partly built vessels, of which Ian's was the only one with any effective resale value. They were, not surprisingly, disinclined to agree to hand over the vessel to Ian or undertake any final works necessary to complete her so that she could be delivered to Spain in time for Ian's annual leave.

Ian began to see his retirement dreams slipping away, so contacted the Royal Yachting Association; they in turn referred him to a solicitor who had, through practical experience, a clear understanding of the competing needs of the parties and a good fax machine. The solicitor also had an understanding wife, who did not object to her husband sitting in bed in the middle of the night having long-distance phone calls with his client in South America.

What the law says

The standard build contract specifically contemplates problems with builders getting into financial difficulties part-way through the construction of a vessel. Accordingly, it contains a number of clauses, the practical effects of which result in the customer acquiring ownership of the vessel and her gear as each part is brought into the boatyard and assembled in the course of her manufacture.

Unfortunately this contract, being between only the manufacturer and the customer, does not properly cover situations such as this one where the works are carried out by a third party or where the goods ordered and paid for have not been delivered to the builder. Accordingly, Ian cannot rely upon these clauses in the contract to demand the release of the vessel from the subcontractors, or the trailer and engine from the suppliers.

While the company is clearly in breach of the contract in failing to provide the completed vessel, Ian's only remedy against them is to sue for breach of contract, at the same time seeking an order for delivery of the launch and the gear; but in view of the subcontractors' legal rights, this would probably achieve little. A further concern here was that, once the company went into liquidation, the liquidators could in theory move against the subcontractors to release both Ian's vessel and the other vessels on the grounds that they were assets of the company and therefore liable to be sold and the proceeds used to pay off the company debts.

While it could be argued that once the vessel came into the hands of the company's liquidators it would, according to the terms of the build contract, automatically become Ian's property, the practical difficulties of persuading liquidators to surrender assets in these circumstances must not be understated.

What, then, is the position of the subcontractors in this matter? Are they entitled to retain the vessel as against the company and Ian? Section 41 of the Sale of Goods Act 1979 provides that the builder has a lien for unpaid purchase money, which effectively enables him to retain possession of the vessel in cases where the full price is not paid or the purchaser becomes insolvent. Accordingly, the subcontractors are perfectly entitled to retain possession of the vessel and refuse to release her to either the company or Ian until their bill is paid in full, provided that the work on the vessel has been effectively completed; indeed, retention of the vessel in this situation is historically the subcontractors' best recourse.

So far as the equipment suppliers are concerned, they too had only contracted with the company and thus Ian could not claim against them directly for the release of the items or for the repayment of the part of the purchase monies that had been paid without pursuing his claim through the company in receivership.

Ian was therefore placed in an extremely difficult position, made all the worse by the need to ensure that the vessel was removed from the UK within seven days of effective completion (commencing from the date of the signed build certificate).

The verdict

After considering his position, Ian quickly realised that he had limited scope for manoeuvre. He accepted that the practical prospects of getting back either the £15,000 that he had paid in part payments, or the completed vessel from the company's receivers, were non-existent. He further wisely came to the conclusion that the removal of the vessel from the subcontractors' premises at the earliest possible date was highly desirable just in case the company receiver decided to pay the subcontractors' unpaid account (which was considerably less than the value of the vessel) and gain possession of Ian's boat with a view to selling it to realise funds by adopting the old legal maxim 'possession is nine-tenths of the law'.

The subcontractors were equally aware of the fact that, while they could retain the boat, they could not dispose of her under the terms of their lien. They were therefore as anxious as Ian to get her off their premises so as to enable them to get on with other paying work. Fortunately, the liquidators appreciated that they were going to have an argument on their hands if they sought to spend what little monies had been gathered in from the company in pursuing any claims to the vessel or the gear. Accordingly, a compromise was agreed between the parties, whereby Ian paid two-thirds of the outstanding sums owed by the company to the subcontractors, who waived the balance of their fees both against Ian and the company; the subcontractors then completed the final outstanding works to Ian's solicitor's satisfaction, and also undertook to carry out various extra works for no charge while fully assisting and co-operating in the vessel being removed from the UK within the seven-day period provided.

The liquidators further agreed to write to the equipment suppliers authorising them to retain the company's payments on account for the engine and trailer, and Ian paid the balance due to each of them so that the items were released in time to be taken abroad with the vessel.

Eventually, Ian ended up paying £6,000 over the contract price but, faced with the prospect of writing off the £15,000 that he had already paid and pursuing a claim against the worthless company in liquidation, he considered that he had made the best of what had potentially been an extremely bad job.

The lessons to be learnt are as follows:

1   Ensure that as far as possible any build contracts are entered into with the persons who are actually carrying out the works, so that payments are made directly to the builders as opposed to an intermediary.

2   If this is not possible, ensure from the outset that you are provided with a full set of receipted invoices from any subcontractors at all stages of the transaction so that you can be sure that the payments are being passed on.

3   If extra equipment is to be provided, then it is best to make the payments directly to the manufacturers or supplier or, alternatively, agree with the builder/supplier that payment for these items will only be made to them upon sight of a receipted invoice and, if possible, delivery note so that you know that the items have been paid for and delivered to the builder before parting with your money.

4   If you cannot arrange to visit the builder personally during the course of construction in order to see the vessel taking shape before your eyes, then give serious consideration to appointing a qualified surveyor to oversee the construction. This need not cost too much and, as well as sometimes resulting in a better end product (on the basis that a fresh approach to certain problems that inevitably arise during the vessel's construction can sometimes be identified), may mean that the 'alarm bells ring before the fire takes hold'.

Case **28 Undischarged and undiscovered**

The facts

In Case 15 we referred to the problems Charles experienced when purchasing a second-hand cruiser. Although it was registered under Part 1 of the Merchant Shipping Act, he only later discovered that there was an undischarged debt against his boat that could well have cost him dearly. Charles was in fact lucky. He could have lost £25,000, but by an extraordinary chain of coincidences we managed to trace the vendor in Spain, where he was living on another boat. The next time this vendor returned to the UK, the police were waiting for him. He was arrested, charged with obtaining pecuniary advantage by deception, and then tried and convicted. It was not his first escapade, so the court decided he should be given the maximum sentence of five years. This vendor had certain assets in Spain which, under a court order, were sold so that the debt to the Easy Finance Company was discharged.

Regrettably, there are many purchasers of second-hand boats who have not been as fortunate as Charles and, although paying the full purchase price for the boat, have ended up losing the vessel as a result of a registered charge by a lender recorded under Part 1 of the Merchant Shipping Act.

We have received many calls on our Helpline service from purchasers of vessels who have experienced similar problems. In most cases the vendors cannot be traced, and the new owner ends up either agreeing to discharge the debt on the vessel, or losing the vessel altogether. There are various risks in purchasing a vessel that is not registered under Part 1 of the Merchant Shipping Act.

The Small Ships Register (SSR), until recently supervised by the RYA, was set up originally to allow boat owners to take vessels out of the UK that were not registered under Part 1 of the Merchant Shipping Act. The intention of the SSR was to satisfy foreign authorities that the keeper/owner of a boat had a recognised authority to use the vessel in a foreign country.

In one of the previous case studies, we may have given the impression that the SSR is a proof of ownership. This is not so, and can be paralleled with the registration of a British motor vehicle that records a keeper who is not necessarily the owner.

We had a case recently where a man called Ian purchased, through a broker, a vessel that was not registered under Part 1 of the Merchant Shipping Act. The vessel was registered with the SSR in the name of the vendor. After carrying out the normal structural survey, Ian agreed to buy the vessel at £85,000 – subject to survey, of course.

On receiving the survey report, Ian came to an agreement with the vendor, via the broker, to buy the vessel for £82,000. Ian and the broker were satisfied that there was no legal charge against the vessel, and the deal was completed in accordance with the ABYA rules. A few months later, Ian heard from the finance company that they had a charge on the vessel. Not so, said Ian, who immediately contacted us. We informed him that, as the debt against the vessel had not been formally registered under Part 1 of the Merchant Shipping Act, the finance company could only have a claim against the original owner, who in this case was quite clearly in breach of contract.

Where a vessel is still in the ownership of a client of a lender, then the lender can legally claim a charge on that vessel. However, if the lender's client disposes of the vessel without the knowledge of the lender, the only redress the lender has is to recover the amount owed by the client. The lender cannot then attempt to secure a charge against the vessel.

Regrettably, in this case, the lender had not registered his interest with the Registrar of British Ships (Part 1, Merchant Shipping Act) and, as soon as the owner of the vessel sold it, the lender lost any legal claim it might have had on the vessel.

Had the owner of the vessel been party to a hire-purchase agreement with the lender, the lender would naturally have a claim on the boat, and repossess it accordingly. Under any form of hire-purchase agreement, the hire-purchase company would normally register its interest with hire purchase investigations. So, should the owner wish to sell the vessel, the vessel would be subject to a hire-purchase investigation.

It is a great pity that there is not a central agency with the ability to record any loans or mortgages given on the security of a named boat. If there was such an agency, the position of a yacht broker, finance house, marine mortgage company, bank or purchaser would be far more secure, as any intending purchaser of a vessel would ensure that, prior to purchase, any debts on the vessel would have to be disclosed and therefore discharged prior to purchase.

A central registration of debts against a vessel has been tried before, but failed from a lack of support by the finance houses, brokers and various other parties.

To prevent this type of fraud increasing, and to protect innocent parties – including the boat buyer, the broker and the finance house – the UK must have a centralised agency that records encumbrances on all types of boat, registered or unregistered. A cross-referencing system would record the name, make and model of the boat, the name of the owner, the name of the lender, and the amount of the encumbrance. A single phone call could then prevent considerable heartache and financial loss.

Case **29 Negligence – but whose?**

The facts

This is the case of an unfortunate sequence of events that could befall any boat owner on a bad day. Howard and Jane had managed to pay off their house mortgage and, as they enjoyed their holidays on Howard's brother's 36 ft fast cruiser, they decided to buy a similar one.

Contact was made with the south coast agent and, three weeks later, their new cruiser was ready for delivery. Howard, his brother Jim, and Jane decided to deliver the boat themselves to a marina on the east coast where Howard had managed to rent a berth for six months.

Armed with the bare essentials for the voyage, they arrived at the agent's yard. After the acceptance trials, and completion of the various formalities, the boat was theirs. As the weather was good, they decided to leave late afternoon, bound eastwards. On leaving the agent's berth, over-enthusiasm on going astern resulted in Jim doing a neat forward somersault over the pulpit into the water, but luckily, apart from dented pride and much amusement to onlookers, no damage was done that a stiff whisky and a change of clothes couldn't cure.

The first part of the passage eastwards was uneventful, with the cruiser attaining an average speed of 25 knots plus. At sundown, Howard throttled back to 16 knots and went inshore to cheat the tide. Just after midnight, there was a sickening thud and both engines stopped dead and, on inspection, the dreaded lobster pot buoy was bouncing against the transom. Howard decided to drop anchor, but to his dismay saw the chain end slip through the bow roller.

As the wind was beginning to increase from the south, Howard put out a Pan signal and soon a nearby fishing boat responded. Quite correctly, Howard agreed a fee with the fishing boat to tow him in to the nearest port.

Five minutes before the fishing boat hove into view, Howard's and Jane's vessel was bumping on the rocks. The fishing boat was unable to get close enough to take Howard's line, but the skipper suggested launching the cruiser's dinghy and outboard and collecting a suitable line from the fishing boat. This was undertaken successfully, and soon the fishing boat had a hold on the cruiser. After some frightening crunching sounds, the fishing boat pulled the cruiser clear. On inspection, the hull appeared intact, although there was a minor leak beneath the cockpit sole.

Once in deep water, the fishing boat shortened the towline and made passage towards the nearest port. Just after entry into the approach channel, the fishing boat went hard aground and the cruiser ploughed heavily into its stern causing considerable damage, both to its bows and rails, and also to the fishing boat. Very soon, the local lifeboat took the cruiser in tow and placed it in a secure berth in the harbour. The fishing boat soon floated off on the tide, and entered the harbour under its own steam.

The following day, Howard's and Jane's boat was lifted ashore where serious damage to the stern gear and bottom was discovered. Howard contacted his insurance company.

This case presents numerous problems as to areas of responsibility:

1 Should the lobster pot marker buoy have been more visible? Should Howard have been motoring through an area, known for its lobster pots, at 16 knots in darkness?
2 Were the boatbuilders negligent in not securing the chain end? Quite clearly, had Howard been able to anchor effectively, little if any damage would have been sustained by his vessel.
3 It was later discovered that the depths in the entrance channel were approximately 3 ft above the declared depths stated. Could the Harbour Board or the hydrographer to the Navy be responsible for the misinformation on the chart? Had the depths been as stated, then clearly the fishing boat could have towed the cruiser into the harbour without running aground.

What the law says

As is so often the case in life, Howard's and Jane's predicament stems from the actions of a number of people and there are, as ever, a bewildering variety of legal implications in the steps played by the various parties.

Dealing firstly with the matter of the lobster pot marker buoy, consideration will have to be given as to whether Howard was negligent in navigation, and of particular relevance here will be consideration of the visibility, Howard's knowledge of the likelihood of the buoys being present, and any marking on the charts that may have suggested that this was an area where fishing floats were likely to be encountered.

If visibility at the time was generally good, and there were no such factors as could reasonably draw Howard's attention to the dangers, then the likelihood is that his insurance company would have to accept that there was no negligence on his part, although there is some uncertainty as to whether speedboat clauses would cover damage sustained as a result of striking the lobster pot. This would not apply to consequential damage caused after the vessel struck the rocks, and therefore there is no point here giving further consideration to this aspect of the matter.

What then is the position regarding the fishermen who laid the lobster pot? The law of the sea provides that, while vessels are entitled to free passage on the high seas, they are also open to all for fishing, but any person who obstructs the free passage of vessels on the high seas can be held liable for the consequences of their obstruction. Clearly, the placing of unlit lobster pots could result in the fishermen in question attracting liability if it could be shown that the pots had been laid across the channel or other navigation lanes and, as such, were reasonably likely to cause such obstruction. In practice, while statutory bodies are empowered by local Acts to legislate as to obstruction of navigation lanes in coastal waters, there is little effective regulation of inshore waters at present, and the practical problems of proving ownership (and hence responsibility) of the fishing pot in question would cause Howard or his insurers a considerable headache.

Going on to consider the position with the anchor chain, clearly the boatyard who supplied the vessel is required by law to provide a vessel that is 'fit for the purposes intended', and this extends to her gear. Here there is clear evidence of negligence in that the chain was not properly connected to the hull and, accordingly, the boatyard can be liable for the resultant damage; however, there will obviously be some argument as to the extent to which the damage resulted from the unsecured chain, as opposed to the other factors.

There is also the question as to whether Howard shares any responsibility in respect of the chain. This again would depend on the extent to which Howard made an inspection of the vessel during the acceptance trial. If (as is normally the case) the bitter end of the chain was at the bottom of an inaccessible chain locker, then it is difficult to see that Howard could be held liable for not having spotted this matter. The reader should, however, note that this is not an altogether unusual state of affairs and, upon taking delivery of a vessel, it is always sensible to check this point (and preferably to do an actual inspection of the connection point in the chain locker).

What then of the position regarding the involvement of the fishing boat? It is important to consider whether the fishing boat's services amount to towage or salvage. The difference is critical here, and it is therefore useful to examine the position carefully. While Howard has clearly agreed a towage fee with the fishing vessel in certain circumstances, what can start out as an agreed towage can become a salvage situation, in which case the tug/salvors may be entitled to considerably more than the simple towage fee. To achieve a salvage situation, there are four specific requirements:

1 There must be marine property involved (ie a ship or cargo or wreckage).

2 The service must be voluntary (ie not by virtue of an existing salvage agreement).
3 There must be a rescue from danger.
4 The service must be successful.

Here, if the fishing vessel had agreed to tow Howard's and Jane's boat, but in the course of such towage the line had broken and the vessel subsequently grounded, then even if the fishing vessel thereafter recovered the vessel from the rocks, the contract between the parties could still amount to a towage contract; towage contracts normally commence once the line is taken aboard the tug. At the time of the fishing vessel coming into sight to effect the tow, Howard's and Jane's vessel was effectively on the rocks, and therefore it would appear likely that, whatever may have been agreed prior to this point, passing of the line amounted to an act of salvage, in which case the fishing vessel would be entitled to a share in the value of Howard's and Jane's cruiser as a salvage award.

This may not be as disadvantageous to Howard and Jane as you may initially think, since it has long been the case that negligent salvors, who in salvaging the vessel cause it damage, can be ordered to forgo their claims.

This is particularly relevant as regards the manner in which the fishing vessel sought to enter the harbour at night. If the vessel was a local vessel, then the skipper should have been aware of the actual depth of the water in the harbour approaches and, in coming in at speed with a tow in this fashion, there is considerable scope for arguing that he displayed a degree of negligence. Alternatively, if the fishing vessel was not a local vessel, then prudence would have dictated that the skipper should have relied upon his echo sounder, in conjunction with charts, in order to avoid grounding and the subsequent collision.

In either event, the suggestion of the speed of the impact, combined with the surrounding circumstances, would seem to suggest that there was poor seamanship on the part of the salvor, which would give considerable weight to arguing that the fishing vessel's salvage fees should be substantially reduced (or mitigated altogether) to reflect the damage caused to the cruiser by the grounding and collision.

There are also some prospects for arguing whether the salvage has ultimately been successful. This makes an interesting comparison with the position where there is a simple towage contract, since it is generally held that the tug is under the control and supervision of the tow, and therefore the tow is primarily responsible for any damage caused *by* the tug and, arguably, *to* the tug in the ensuing collision. It is of further interest to note that a towage fee is only payable when the contract service has been provided. If the service fails, no money is payable. What then of the RNLI?

While it is true that the RNLI has undoubtedly rendered the service that could amount to salvage, in general the RNLI crews are not inclined to make such claims, although there is no legal reason why they cannot do so.

To the extent that the accident was contributed to by the incorrect soundings, a Harbour Board is under a statutory duty to ensure that all reasonable steps are taken to make navigation within the harbour safe, which includes the provision of buoyage and other navigational aids. If a ship is damaged by running on to a sandbank that has been inadequately marked, then a number of decisions have resulted in the harbour authorities being held liable.

The Harbour Board is also under a responsibility to properly check and sound the harbour and dredge the channels, so if these duties have not been properly carried out by the Harbour Board and/or its servants or agents, this could result in a claim against the harbour authorities being upheld.

The verdict

Howard's insurers had a spirited argument with the skipper of the fishing vessel who sought salvage. Eventually a settlement was made whereby the skipper of the fishing vessel received an agreed sum which reflected his responsibility for the damage to Howard's and Jane's boat arising out of the grounding at the harbour mouth. The insurers made this payment primarily out of a desire to ensure that any salvor's efforts, whether successful or otherwise, were to be encouraged.

This fishing vessel's skipper reported the misinformation on the chart in somewhat Anglo Saxon terms to the Harbour Board, which is still conducting its own enquiries into the matter. Howard's and Jane's insurers reached a further agreement with the builders whereby the costs of the cruiser's repairs were borne jointly. Howard and Jane now endeavour to avoid areas where lobster pot buoys are to be seen and have taken the sensible precaution of purchasing a large kedge anchor with sufficient chain and cable to avoid the problem recurring in the future.

Case **30 Insured peril or design defect?**

The facts

Although costly, boating for the majority is a most pleasurable pastime. Unfortunately, at Ward & McKenzie we tend to hear only of the more unhappy side of the activity. In our opinion, no case has been so grossly unfair as the following one.

Dr J is a highly acclaimed neuro-surgeon with a successful practice operating from his consulting rooms in Harley Street. The doctor has enjoyed many years of boating with his family in his trusty Grand Banks, and holidays have included cruising to Scandinavia and down the Rhein. After consultation with his wife, it was decided to sell the Grand Banks and replace it with a larger, faster craft.

They went to all the boat shows and soon a shortlist of suitable vessels was drawn up. The doctor was attracted to one supplier, who offered to take his Grand Banks in part exchange; soon a deal was struck and a building contract entered into. The doctor was not happy with the standard specified engines so asked if larger engines of another make could be installed. The supplier was happy to do this, although he explained that they had not previously installed this type of engine in any of their vessels. However, the supplier soon provided an estimate for the additional costs.

This estimate was accepted by the doctor and, six months later, his new acquisition was ready for sea trials and delivery. The 45-minute sea trial went successfully, with the only apparent fault being the echo sounder – which totally failed to work. The boatyard agreed to replace this, and much champagne flowed on that sunny Saturday morning after our doctor had settled the final invoice.

Two weeks later the doctor and his holiday crew left their south coast port bound for Ostend; they planned to cruise the Baltic, taking advantage of the long daylight hours. Their trip would have taken them up the Dutch coast, and ultimately through thc Keil Canal into thc Baltic. They arrived in Ostend just in time to catch the lock into the Mercator Marina. The boat had behaved admirably, averaging a speed well in excess of expectations. A good meal was had by all in one of the many quayside fish restaurants that Ostend is noted for.

The following morning dawned bright and clear, with a good forecast. At 10 am they were powering across the Sheldt Estuary when there was an almighty explosion from below. The doctor immediately shut down his engines and raced down the flybridge ladder. By the time he reached the aft deck, the saloon was ablaze and the majority of the hatch boards had blown out. The heat was too intense even to consider a fire extinguisher – besides which, they were positioned at the other end of the fire. The doctor was aware of the risks of a further explosion and ordered his crew to launch the liferaft and abandon the vessel. There was not even enough time to send out a mayday or discharge any distress signals. Luckily, no one was hurt and the evacuation into the liferaft proved easier than expected.

Within minutes, a large salvage tug appeared from nowhere. The doctor and his crew were rescued from the raft, and the raft was lifted on board and deflated. The tug then went in close to the stricken vessel and the foam cannon extinguished the flames in seconds. The charred remains were then taken in tow bound for Flushing. On arrival, customs, police and a representative of the Harbour Authority were waiting. The ship's papers, and the doctor's and crew's personal effects, were still aboard the burnt-out wreck. To add insult to injury, the harbour authorities taped a notice to the doctor's boat stating that it had to be removed from the dock within 48 hours.

After filling in numerous forms, the doctor rang his insurance company and they informed him that their surveyor would be travelling from Sheerness to Flushing on the next ferry. The doctor met the surveyor off the ferry and took him to the boat. After inspecting the remains, the surveyor was not forthcoming, but gave the doctor a claim form to fill in. This was duly completed and handed back to the surveyor. Arrangements were made with a local scrapyard that the boat should be lifted ashore and stored, salvaging as far as possible all the valuable items such as engines, generator, rudders, stern gear, etc.

Two days after his return to England, the doctor received a letter from his insurance company stating that, in the opinion of the surveyor, the explosion and resultant fire had been caused by a serious design defect and that, under the Institute Yacht Clauses, this was not considered as an insured peril. The writer further suggested that the doctor should levy a claim against the supplier/manufacturer. Taking this advice, he contacted the supplier/manufacturer, only to find that this firm had gone into liquidation 10 days previously. Not knowing what to do, the doctor then contacted us.

What the law says

The contract for the construction of a boat is a contract for the sale of goods – or, rather, an agreement to sell the goods which becomes a contract of sale when certain conditions are satisfied. For example, the usual standard form of contract for the construction of a vessel provides that the buyer gets property to the materials used in the boat's construction as and when those materials are actually used. Although the engines installed were larger than the standard engines installed in this type of boat, the doctor, quite reasonably, could rely on the expertise, judgement and advice of the supplier who stated that 'although we have not installed this type of engine previously, we feel satisfied that we can adhere to your requirements without any problem'.

In previous case studies we have introduced the Sale of Goods Act 1979, and particularly Section 14 which implies certain terms into contracts made between individuals and those acting in the course of business. Those terms require that the goods provided are of merchantable quality and reasonably fit for their required purpose. Although the engine specification had changed, this makes no difference to the legal requirement of the supplier to supply a boat that is of merchantable quality and fit for its required purpose. Quite clearly, it would appear that the doctor's boat was not so, and therefore the supplier was in breach of an implied term.

On advice, the doctor decided not to pursue his insurance company, but to consider the other options open to him. As he had technically accepted the vessel, he would have difficulty in proving his rejection to a court. The Sale of Goods Act states that if a buyer accepts goods, then he cannot afterwards reject them, but he must instead claim damages for any losses he has suffered. However, the Act also states that a buyer is not deemed to have accepted goods until he has exercised his right to examine them to see that they conform to the contract.

The defect in the doctor's boat was latent and required several hours of use prior to manifestation (the insurance company's surveyor established that the heat from an exhaust elbow had ignited the integral GRP fuel tank, which ultimately ruptured, thus causing the explosion). Even if the doctor could successfully prove his right to reject, there would be very little hope of recovering any money from the supplier, who was in receivership. The doctor would just stand in line with all the other creditors. The only course of action that the doctor could take was to sue the supplier/manufacturer for negligence.

The verdict

Fortunately, the supplier/builder of the boat had engaged the services of a naval architect to draw up the revised engine installation plans for the boat and, like most naval architects, he was covered by his professional indemnity. The liquidator very quickly picked up this point and, after many months of frustration and many letters, the architect's insurers agreed to pay 60 per cent of the doctor's claim. Although the doctor was £50,000 out of pocket, he decided that he was not prepared to take the risk of suing the architect direct.

Note: The architect had no contractual responsibility to the doctor, but only a contractual responsibility to the supplier/manufacturer. The architect's insurers were aware of this and realised that the only claim that could be levied against them would be by the boat supplier/manufacturer's liquidator. The doctor could, in fact, have sued the supplier and in turn the liquidator could then have sued the architect. The doctor, quite reasonably, decided against this chain of action and to cut his losses.

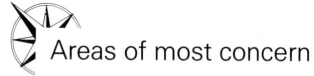

Areas of most concern

All the case studies here have reported on specifics. As a result of our Helpline service, I can outline those areas that seem to concern the boat owner the most:

Insurance companies and underwriters failing to honour a claim

In Case 17 we reported on the case of Gavin and Jane who had sold up everything to buy a charter yacht in the Mediterranean. After a period of time, the business failed and the bank stepped in. While visiting relatives in England, Gavin and Jane heard that their vessel (and home) had sunk on her berth. Gavin naturally made a claim to his insurance company and, after a period of time, they replied that they were not satisfied with the validity of the claim and, on that basis, were not prepared to pay out. The insurance company realised that Gavin was in no financial position to pursue the matter through the court, until they heard that he had legal aid. Immediately, the insurance company changed their tune and wanted to discuss a settlement. Luckily, an acceptable settlement was arrived at, much to Gavin's and Jane's relief.

We have received numerous calls on our Helpline service from boat owners in very similar predicaments. We heard of a sad tale of poor Steve, who returned his boat on its trailer to the agent so that certain warranty work could be carried out. As Steve was a working man, he could only deliver the boat on a Sunday evening and, knowing that the agent's boatyard would be locked, made arrangements with the foreman to leave the boat just outside the gates and put all the necessary keys through the letterbox. Steve immobilised the boat by chaining one wheel to the concrete fence post and another back around the trailer.

The following morning the agents rang up to say that the boat was not there. Steve immediately informed the police and his insurance company. Several weeks later, and after several statements had been made by Steve to the insurance assessor, he received a letter from the insurance company outlining that within the policy there was a clause stating that any vessel left in a public place must be adequately secured and immobilised. The very fact that the vessel had been stolen meant that adequate precautions had not been taken, and on that basis the insurance company were not prepared to settle Steve's claim. One has to question seriously the ethics of the insurance company in this matter, for they could argue that the very fact that the boat was stolen means that it was not adequately secured.

Then there was Dave who, after a row with his wife, decided to spend the night on his boat. Unfortunately, while preparing his evening meal, his chip pan caught fire. He used the fire extinguisher adjacent to the galley, but that only made matters worse. He grabbed another fire extinguisher from the wheelhouse and used that. However, in a frighteningly quick time, the whole galley was ablaze. Nervous about explosion, Dave abandoned his boat to seek help. The boat burnt out and was a total loss.

Dave put in a claim to his insurance company; they replied that, in the opinion of the insurance company's surveyor, the fire fighting appliances were not of adequate size for the boat and were not suitably positioned. On that basis and in respect of a clause in his policy, they were therefore not prepared to meet the claim.

I must make it clear that, in our area of work, we only hear the bad stories; but of course, as in all walks of life, there are the good and the not so good. There are many reputable insurance companies, but a boat owner can only really assess his particular company after he has made the claim. Our advice is to shop around and make sure you have the policy that you want and that you fully understand and comply with the various requirements that are set out in its terms.

The purchase of a secondhand boat privately

Many people buy boats privately, as in most cases they are cheaper as a result of the fact that the vendor does not have to pay a broker's commission.

In Case 15 we saw that Charles had purchased a motor yacht privately, only to find after four months that a writ was placed on it for £25,000 by the mortgage company. By pure chance, we discovered the vendor living on the Costa del Sol. On his return to England to see his family, needless to say the police were waiting for him at Gatwick. He was arrested, charged with obtaining pecuniary advantage by deception, then tried and convicted. It was not his first such escapade, and he was given the maximum sentence of five years. Fortunately, he had certain assets in Spain, and those were sold to enable the mortgage on the boat to be discharged.

We also heard from Nigel who had unwittingly bought a stolen vessel, spent a fortune on fitting it out, only for it to be returned to its rightful owner several months later. Luckily the owner was a reasonable man, and offered to pay a proportion of the fit-out costs.

If you are buying a boat privately, you should have no problems as to title and information on any encumbrance if the boat is registered under Part 1 of the Merchant Shipping Act. However, do make an enquiry to the Registrar of British Ships; it is well worth the nominal fee. Also check around the boatyard or marina to find out whether there are any outstanding mooring fees or yard bills. Ensure you have sight of the registration document prior to parting with any money, and satisfy yourself that the registered owner and his address is the same as that on the bill of sale.

Buying an unregistered boat, though, is a totally different matter, and our recommendation is always to hand the purchase arrangements over to a qualified person or, if you can establish a satisfactory price, a broker. They will know all the pitfalls of buying an unregistered boat.

The Small Ships Register is intended to give proof of ownership. However, it does not record any charge a third party might have on a boat. If you wish to pursue the purchase arrangements yourself, then we recommend the following:

(*a*) Inspect the bill of sale, making sure that the person you are going to hand the money over to is the same as the name of the person recorded on the bill of sale – and watch out for forged bills of sale.

(*b*) Contact the original owner to establish that a legitimate sale took place.

(*c*) Contact the vendor's bank and establish whether or not the boat has been used for collateral.

(*d*) Ask around the boatyard or marina to find out whether or not the vendor pays his mooring fees and yard bills promptly, and if there are any outstanding bills deduct them from the purchase price and pay them direct.

(*e*) Go to the vendor's house and satisfy yourself that he is one and the same, and also make a cross reference with the electoral register.

(*f*) Contact as many marine finance houses as possible to ascertain whether or not a loan has been made on the boat. (If a vessel is under a certain value, many finance houses do not insist that the vessel be registered under Part 1 of the Merchant Shipping Act prior to giving a loan on the vessel.) This area gives us great concern as it is virtually impossible for a prospective purchaser to satisfy himself or herself that the vessel is free of all encumbrance. However, within the bill of sale, the vendor agrees that the vessel is sold free of all encumbrance.

(*g*) Be cautious if the vendor wants to rush the deal or gives a discount for immediate payment.

There are a few firms that specialise in private boat purchase and, for the sake of a few hundred pounds, it is well worth the peace of mind. However, ensure that they have professional indemnity and, if necessary, ask to see their certificate. Be cautious of using any firm, or firm of surveyors, that does not have professional indemnity, as professional indemnity can only be gained by experience and qualification.

Boatyard estimates

In Case 7 we covered the matter of Jan, who asked several boatyards to quote for the refitting of his classic motor yacht. The estimates varied considerably, and Jan accepted the lowest estimate that was given by a boatyard well known for this type of refit work. Jan, who lived in Norway, made all the stage payments. However, when he came to collect his vessel, he was horrified to find that the final bill brought the total cost of the refit to approximately three times that of the estimate that was given. After certain deliberations, the boatyard agreed that he could pay the difference between the original estimate and the invoice total into an Escrow Account. Unless this had been agreed quite clearly, the boatyard would not have released his vessel. Fortunately, the case went to arbitration and the arbitrator studied all the relevant invoices and time sheets. He confirmed Jan's view that there had been considerable over-charging and held that Jan should pay only 15 per cent more than the original estimate.

This is quite a frequent problem and on many occasions we have worked into the small hours perusing time sheets and equipment/ material schedules.

Unfortunately, in most cases boatyards will only give estimates and not fixed price quotations, as they argue that they are not sure what is entailed. If you require work to be done on your boat, shop around the various boatyards – but remember to take into account any delivery costs of the vessel, etc. Regrettably, certain boatyards have a policy of giving exceptionally low estimates on the basis of 'a sprat to catch a mackerel', knowing full well that once they have their hands on your boat it will not be returned until the final bill has been settled. Their arguments are always the same: there was far more wrong with the boat than was apparent at first; the job was more difficult than they had originally envisaged; and of course it was only an estimate.

Beware of unusually low estimates, and ask for an itemised estimate so that you can keep a check during the works. Insist that the boatyard inform you in writing in respect of any particular item that might exceed the estimate, and then allow for this. Watch out for hidden extras, such as storage, insurance, plant hire, etc. If possible, use a boatyard that is a member of the British Marine Industry's Federation and ensure that their standard contract is utilised.

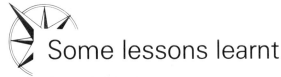

Some lessons learnt

Dear Mr Ward,

The last 18 months have probably been the most eventful in our sailing lives, full of adventure, challenge and disappointment. It is difficult to believe that so much could happen in such a short space of time – the near fulfilment of a boyhood dream, a dramatic and record breaking air-sea rescue, and the unbelievable pain of near financial ruin.

Entering the Two Handed Transatlantic Race was the fulfilment of plans made some 20 years ago in the playground of a small school in the Midlands. Simon and I have spent a lifetime sailing together, loving to spend our spare time sailing and boating. We have progressed through many different classes of boats from those early days in our Mirror dinghy to large ocean-going yachts.

My love of the sea took me into a career as a professional seaman in the Royal Navy where, as seaman officer with a Bridge Watchkeeping ticket, I served on ships of all sizes around the world.

The commitment, planning and organisation required to enter a long distance ocean race is quite staggering. Many people have been quoted as saying that the hardest part is to get the boat ready at the start line, and we certainly found this to be true. Planning started some two years before the start date: the rules of qualification are, quite rightly, very strict and exacting with regard to both the standard of the boat and the experience of the crew. Our qualifying sail was completed in our original race boat, a 33 ft sloop, during a cruise to the Baltic covering 1,800 nautical miles in just 24 days.

When visiting some Dutch sailing friends on our return, we were introduced to the current manufacturer of our boat. We were impressed by their new vessel, a ULDB design with an excellent racing pedigree. Weighing up the cost of the race refit necessary on our own vessel, we decided to spend the money on this newer boat with top-quality equipment.

A deal was struck whereby a Dutch broker gave us a fall back price on our vessel. To cut a long story short, the broker neglected the boat and the deal fell through. Urgently in need of a new boat for the race, we settled on another type from a British manufacturer. Again, we were to be disappointed in that, having agreed a deal and had the boat surveyed, we were gazumped two days before taking delivery. We were now getting even closer to the start date without a boat, and a search was made in earnest to find something suitable.

We essentially wanted a fast, foreign, strong cruising boat that would be suitable for the race. Our attention was drawn to a boat whose lines we had long admired. The advertising literature quoted the boat as being 'Ideal for longer trips, fully crewed or short-handed, it is a pleasure to sail. The technology that has gone into this boat offers the highest degree of reliability and safety.' This was supported by the fact that every boat is provided with a German-isher Lloyd series production certificate, which the builders claim as 'your guarantee of consistent high quality of all our yachts'. We spoke to the UK importer and discussed our needs for the race. They recommended the boat and put us in touch with their agents in the North East, who had a boat in stock. We seriously considered buying a new British boat, but the foreign boat had the advantage of a slightly favourable price and 'immediate availability'.

The purchase was to become a total nightmare.

Things started to go wrong almost immediately. When we arrived to take delivery of the boat after an eight-hour drive to the North East, we found it trapped by other boats at the far end of the boatyard, still out of the water, and still having work done to it. In fact, not only were there numerous things still to be done, but much of the work that had been completed was either of poor quality or simply wrong. One look at the newly fitted lee cloths that stood a meagre 4 inches above the cushions left us with a sinking feeling in our stomachs.

It was clear from the boat's position in the yard, the late time of day, and the low state of tide, that there was no way that the boat could possibly be launched. Anyway, this was hypothetical since there was so much still to do and to put right. Particularly galling was the fact that knowing the delivery date could not be met, they had not even had the courtesy to let us know. The quite pathetic inadequacy of the lee cloths left us wondering what knowledge they had of boats. This feeling was exacerbated by the aggressive attitude of the company's divisional managing director. He even came close to showing his fists when we explained that there was no way we were accepting the boat in its current condition.

We were left sitting in our car in a cold boatyard as it gradually got darker, with all but a few workmen going home for a Bank Holiday weekend. The managing director eventually calmed down and listened to what we had to say. He then went to have a look at the boat for himself and returned full of apologies, saying that he would be having very strong words with his workshop manager. He also promised to have the boat delivered to Portsmouth by the following weekend, guaranteeing to check the boat personally. We then spent our first night in our new boat with a yard cradle, rather than salt sea, beneath us. We were given a first-class rail ticket home courtesy of the company, together with a formal apology for the situation; this was small consolation, but nevertheless a gesture that was gratefully received. At this stage, having already trans-ferred the last major payment into their account to 'guarantee' the delivery date, we were unfortunately very much in their hands.

It took them three weeks to get the boat to us. This delay was particularly trying as the start date was getting even closer, and we had much proving to do. We also had a fair amount of our own equipment still to install, and of course the yacht itself had to be qualified for the race. On the plus side, the boat was now in our possession, and with these details completed we would be finally ready for the Big One.

We could reasonably have expected that our troubles were nearly over. In reality, they had only just begun.

On close inspection, we found numerous defects in lots of different areas. We highlighted these to the UK importer who arranged to have them put right – at a cost to us of £600. The UK importer was exceptionally critical of the quality of work of their agents, and their poor adherence to manufacturers' pre-delivery checks. Surely now the worst of our problems were over?

Unfortunately not, as things on the boat started to break almost from day one, and the more we sailed the boat during qualifying, the more problems came to light. After the first night spent at the pile berth, the bow roller had cracked in half and a mooring cleat had pulled out from the deck. The first time we raised the spinnaker, it pulled the track away from the mast. The log and echo sounder did not work, nor the autopilot installation, despite the attention (and £600 bill) from the electronic engineers. The boat leaked, soaking the cushion in the fore cabin. There was also a large pool of water from an unidentified source collecting in the main bilge.

With the boat in Plymouth and only two weeks to go before the start of the race, we pleaded with the agents in the North East to sort the boat out and informed them that we had found local companies willing to tackle the repairs. No help was forthcoming, so we had the repairs carried out elsewhere for another £350.

The morning of the race was tranquil. Blue sky broke through the clouds and a light breeze drifted across the marina. An air of calm surrounded our camp of friends and supporters, yet each of us had our own fears and apprehensions. Our minds were now firmly on the gruelling 3,000 miles ahead of us, with the prospects of mountainous seas, gale force winds, icebergs and dense fog.

I think sometimes in life we drive ourselves down paths with only one way out, where there is no turning back. The question of why one wants to enter a race such as this proves ever difficult to answer, yet for us it is the challenge and the chance to push yourself to the limit. When you analyse what you are doing, it just doesn't seem to make sense. You get in debt to get cold, wet and uncomfortable, for a tenth of the year. We nearly lost our jobs in trying to get the time off work, and will be paying back huge loans for the next five years. I can only surmise that we must be a little mad – yet, for those who have it, the urge to race this vast ocean is unstoppable. The commitment has to be total, and one needs a large dose of 'dedication to the task' to overcome the many difficulties.

The start went well, and we were soon heading west towards the south west approaches, our spinnaker dazzling bright and our log showing a fairly steady 6–7 knots. Daylight slowly faded and the wind came round on to the nose, so we dropped the spinnaker in favour of the number 1 genoa. Throughout the night we stayed very close to *Quixote*, a UFO 34, often being no more than a few boat lengths away.

It was about 5 o'clock the following afternoon that we discovered our problems were far from over. The battery indicator showed moderate to poor and we decided to run the engine to charge the batteries. The engine started, ran rough for a while, and then stopped dead. While investigating the cause, a litre of water came gushing out of the engine air filter. Since we were still relatively close to land, and therefore had the option of effecting repairs to our primary method of battery charging, we set course for Crosshaven in Eire. It is difficult to describe just how we felt; we had given so much to do this race. We had doubled our investment in a boat to get quality and reliability and, almost immediately, our hopes of a good position were dashed.

We phoned the agents and the builders to tell them of the continuing problems with their boat in the wild hope that they might just help us. In what had now become predictable form, a representative of the agents whom we met in Crosshaven had an interesting and revealing response to our pleas for help. When we told him that our engine had been installed incorrectly and was taking on water, his response was 'Good', when we told him that our boat was taking on large quantities of water, his response was 'Good', when we told him that there had been numerous other equipment failures, his reply was yet again 'Good'. It was difficult to avoid the feeling that if we had told him his right trouser leg was on fire, then his reply would have been the same – quite simply he wasn't listening; he wasn't even interested in seeing the boat.

Disappointed that we had yet again been refused even the most basic courtesies and assistance, we effected repairs at our own expense and continued the race. The next five days were to see a continual string of equipment failures, and a deterioration in the general seaworthiness of the vessel. Interestingly, a recent study of the factors influencing seaworthiness came to the following conclusion: 'When considering seaworthiness, it is easy to fall into the trap of looking at a boat as a whole. Ultimately, gauging a yacht's seaworthiness depends largely on her ability to function and it is therefore the combination of dozens of features and pieces of gear that makes the difference. Seaworthiness is directly related to safety. The essence of seaworthiness is a yacht which looks after the crew, who in turn look after her, and therefore themselves.' On this basis, our boat failed the test in every important respect, the next five days seeing a continued deterioration in her condition, with a number of equipment failures and continuing ingress of water. Remember also that this was a two-handed event; almost every equipment failure required the off-watch crew member to climb out of his pit and turn to, further depriving him of sleep and thereby potentially reducing his effectiveness in an emergency.

It was difficult to believe that so many things could break, or cease to function, in such a short period of time. Problems with quality, design and installation became more and more apparent. As the weather worsened, the yacht started to take on considerable quantities of water, the leaks that we had paid so many times to have repaired continued unabated. The extent of the problem was such that the floor boards would again be awash within a few hours of pumping out. The greatest difficulty was in establishing where so much water was coming from.

To have a leak is not too bad if you can find the source, since you can attempt to seal it or, at the very least, be able to monitor it. Our difficulty was that the yacht's internal mouldings prevent the inspection of many areas of the hull, and form a hidden passage for water moving around inside the boat. There was a great pressure of water in between the two mouldings, which caused some of the internal mouldings to bow outwards. The likelihood certainly seemed to be that the leak was in there somewhere, but we just couldn't get in to check. The shallow bilges made the situation worse, being particularly difficult to pump clear, and rendering even the extended hose that we had attached to the ship's bilge pump more or less useless (the hose supplied with the boat would not reach the main bilge). The best way of emptying the bilges, although labour intensive, was via a small portable bilge pump and buckets. We were filling 20 buckets (around 40 gallons) in about four hours at the very worst times. The fore and aft cabins were soaking, giving us the main saloon as the only vaguely habitable place.

Not surprisingly, the vast quantities of water down below eventually took out most of our electrics, including the navigation instruments. Miraculously, the Loran and ssb radio survived, which left us with a comforting link with the outside world. It also enabled us to give accurate position information to the Coastguard when it finally looked as if the boat was not going to support us much longer.

The boat just could not cope with the conditions which, while rough, were not abnormal for the North Atlantic. The self-tacking jib track and mainsheet track bent under the weight of the (reduced/reefed) sails. The heater relies on a chimney screwed into the deck, which actually blew off in the wind, leaving a hole that needed to be filled with a softwood plug.

To prevent the engine from backflooding, we were having to lean over the stern and place another plug in the exhaust outlet – there was no effective siphon break on this boat! The diesel and water tanks' vent pipes did not have swan necks and were vulnerable to the ingress of sea water, contaminating the contents. Soiled water started to flood back through the heads from the holding tank, which we were later to discover was due to incorrect installation of the pipework. Quite remarkably, the main structural bulkhead cracked all the way through. Even the lee cloths failed, dumping my sleeping crew unceremoniously into the sea water that covered the cabin sole, sleeping bag and everything else.

Despite the growing catalogue of failures, the decision to return to the nearest land was probably one of the most difficult either of us has ever had to make. We had put everything into the race and there was a great urge to carry on. Neither of us wanted to be the one to recommend the action to the other, but we both knew it was the only sensible option – common sense and wise seamanship winning over the sheer will to carry on. For the first time in our sailing lives, the boat had become the limiting factor, reaching the limits of endurance before ourselves – and we certainly make no claims to being supermen! We were devastated to have been let down by a boat that we had bought specifically for the event, and that had cost far more than we could really afford. Equipment continued to fail; the engine had stopped working shortly after

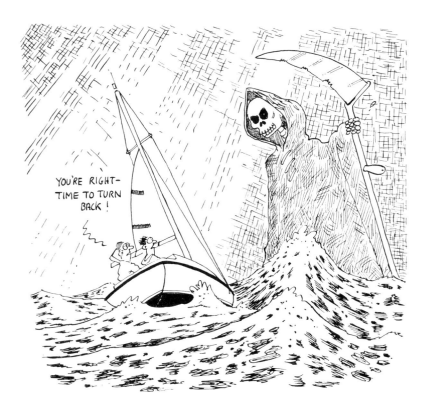

leaving Crosshaven, the genoa halyard had parted as it rounded the block into the mast, the rudder stock had started to squeak badly – a result of incompatible materials in the bushes, which further increased crew fatigue by depriving the off watch crew member of sleep.

By the time we reached the decision to turn for land, we had become seriously concerned about the boat's ability to support our lives. We made an HF call to Falmouth Coastguard, informing him of our position and situation. Our fear was that, in changing to port tack for the return, the water in the bilge would slosh over to the starboard side, where our batteries and main electrical connections were sited. This would increase the probability of losing radio communication, so we felt it was much better to inform the Coastguard of our problems and potential further difficulties in advance. We arranged a transmission schedule with Portishead Radio, enabling them to monitor our progress towards land at hourly intervals, which also had the benefit of serving as an 'alarm' if we failed to call in or respond to their call. The rate at which water gathered in the bilge reduced substantially off the wind, but nevertheless still involved very regular pumping.

The rudder developed an intermittent fault, failing to turn beyond the half lock position to starboard. This later added to the problems by causing a gybe, during which the mainsheet cleared away the actual steering pedestal itself. Following this, we continued under emergency tiller until the steering system failed altogether, jamming on full lock to starboard. This thwarted all our attempts to produce an effective jury rig system, since the jammed rudder always had the upper hand. Following long discussions with the Coastguard regarding our situation, and a couple of knockdowns caused by steep breaking waves, arrangements were made for a helicopter from RAF BRAWDY to airlift us from the stricken vessel some 270 miles west of Ireland. This was an all time record distance for an RAF rescue without refuelling at sea.

The vessel was found by a fishing boat, which attempted to take her in tow. However, as a result of the jammed steering gear, they found the task impossible. The boat was later salvaged by a warship and returned to the UK, where we engaged a surveyor to investigate our list of defects, comprising some 68 items. On close inspection, our surveyor added substantially to this list, and his findings are now detailed in a report covering some 40 pages. As an example, he revealed that the heat-resistant exhaust hosing had been used as the heads' waste pipe, with the original ordinary waste pipe being used instead as the exhaust. The keel and rudder were also not vertical to the centreline and the hull was even concave in places.

To date, we have received no help or support whatsoever from either the manufacturers or their agents. The UK agent denies that there is anything wrong with the boat at all, and seems even more disinterested since they are no longer selling this type of boat. The builders say they have inspected the boat and the only problem is a small leak in the anchor locker, but they maintain that it is absolutely impossible that they could supply a boat with so many defects, and are therefore not willing to even look at it themselves – not even to try and prove themselves right.

There are many lessons to be learnt from the episode, which can be summarised as follows:

1 Do not necessarily trust the supplier/agent. No matter what you think of them as people, or how impeccable their credentials as yachtsmen, remember they are salesmen and therefore will inevitably be biased towards their product, if only through loyalty.

2 Have a new boat surveyed, no matter how unnecessary it may seem. (We were advised by a surveyor that it is not necessary to have a new boat surveyed.) It is true that for most of us the boat will be covered by fair trading and merchantable quality legislation. However, it is of little comfort when you find yourself sinking many miles from land. It is also of little use when, to prove your point, you have to battle your way through the courts with all the attendant costs and delays to your sailing pleasure – which was, after all, the point of the purchase in the first place. A little money now can save a great deal further down the line.

3 Try to insure against faults in manufacture and design. Do not rely on manufacturers' warranties, as they are impossible to enforce in law.

4 Take out comprehensive legal protection insurance to cover legal fees etc, top value £70,000–£80,000. This is not a bad idea in any event; it is not only the marine industry that can suffer from 'sharks', who will work on the basis that most punters will not carry through threats of legal action because of the cost.

5 Do not rely on Germanisher Lloyd-type certificates, particularly 'series production' certificates, such as possessed by the builder. The award of individual hull certificates may give some confidence in the abilities of the manufacturer, but there is no comeback on boats not coming up to the standards set by the classification. BS 5750 may be more comforting, since it applies not just to the hull or production line, but to the company as a whole; it encompasses their original materials, their customer care set up, and even the infrastructure of the company itself. You are, therefore, less likely to suffer from a manufacturer who doesn't want to know once your money is in his bank account.

6 If you intend to go long distances offshore, try to get out in rough conditions inshore first to prove seaworthiness. Remember when testing your 'jury rig' that you may have to compete with the original gear in some circumstances!

7 Take a professional's advice regarding the suitability of equipment, scantlings and other fittings for the use to which you intend to put the vessel.

8 Be prepared to have to wait for two years (or more) to get compensation.

Perhaps the most surprising thing about the entire situation is not the numerous defects – the boat would appear to be a 'Monday morning job' – but the complete and utter lack of support or help that has been offered. Furthermore, it appears that none will be forthcoming unless we bring the full weight of English law to bear upon the suppliers.

We have invited both the agents and manufacturers to meet us and hear first hand about the problems that we have encountered, yet each has declined. Neither will talk to us direct, preferring to hide behind their solicitors and surveyors. Not only have we received no help, but we have had to put up with outright aggression and hostility on a personal level, and even attempts to slur our name in the yachting press.

This is by no means typical of all yacht manufacturers or suppliers. None the less, if you are in the market for a new yacht, my crew and I would urge you strongly to listen to what we are saying before you take out your cheque book. Anyone can make a mistake, even yacht manufacturers; how that mistake is handled can make the difference between ongoing loyalty and litigation.

Many years ago, this poor standard of quality and customer care was the norm in the UK motor industry. These manufacturers, however, saw the advantages to be gained from treating their customers with respect and courtesy, and dragged themselves up to a level of service in which they can have some justifiable pride. Things are not perfect across the whole motor industry, but they recognise this, and work constantly towards improving their service and thereby their image. At the end of the day, life is easier for all concerned. The marine industry now appears to be facing the same choices: continue to ignore the benefits of a happy customer relationship, or take the initiative and profit from improved service.

Many of the subcontractors used by major yacht manufacturers for repair/installation work do not reflect the quality of their products, and this leads to much frustration among their customers. Many of us have spent between three and six times as much on yachts as we have on cars. Is it too much to expect the same level of service? How about franchised servicing within the marine industry?

Food for thought . . .

Yours sincerely,

Piracy – by law **A letter to the author**

Summary

This is a story of a banking group that spotted an outstanding promotional opportunity for its newly formed marine finance division in association with my yacht and its entry in the Whitbread Round the World Race, and went to exceptional lengths in using both pressure and persuasion to involve me in a form of loan agreement that contained a substantial sponsorship element.

While the Race was actually in progress, this banking group decided on a change in policy. Deeming the publicity generated to be no longer necessary, the banking group decided not to pay for it, so leaving me in a very difficult financial position.

Once this group had decided to close down its marine operation, it pursued a ruthless policy of repossession. In my case, this was carried out in clear breach of agreement, but it justified this by legal manoeuvrings that were an affront to the basic principles of British justice. These manoeuvrings were condoned by a judge who had made a decision from which he was determined not to be moved, and would not be inconvenienced by evidence and witnesses. Instead of having a legal battle against a bank, which I could not lose, I was sucked into a battle with the judge, which I could not win. The more the judge was shown to be wrong, the more bizarre his decisions became, and the more farcical the excuses he accepted from the bank.

The story details the wanton legalised dissipation of my assets as my yacht was allowed to deteriorate under arrest, the manner in which this deterioration was covered up, and the proposition that because there would be nothing left for me if I won at a trial, I should not be allowed to have one.

It tells of the refusal of the Lord Chancellor (Lord Hailsham) to intervene in this legal charade, despite representation by my MP; of how the banking group escaped censure by the Finance Houses Association by the simple act of resignation from that body; and of how the regulatory authority, the Bank of England, refused to take any action in spite of the clearest evidence of failure to meet the authorisation criteria prescribed by the Banking Act. It shows that, while the watchdogs allowed the bank to escape, there was no escape for me from the mechanism that 'listed' me as a debtor – which means I cannot borrow money from any normal source of lending. Yet I was – and remain – absolutely innocent of any fault or default whatsoever.

I have included a description of the substantial losses to the shareholders of the banking group, as well as to the taxpayer, as a result of the action. An annexe to this chapter describes some remarkable failures in the system of court transcripts.

Timetable of banking

- In January 1981 I needed to borrow £180,000 to buy out the interest of my former sponsors in my £350,000 racing yacht.
- In February 1981 I was persuaded by the marine manager of a finance house to approach his company; it had been newly acquired by a separate banking organisation and was establishing a marine division.
- In March 1981 the finance loans committee of the bank rejected my loan application, saying that the maximum loan I could service from operation of the yacht would be £120,000. It was agreed that I needed sponsorship for the difference.
- On 25 March 1981 the chief executive of the bank, having identified an outstanding promotional opportunity, offered a loan of £180,000 on non-commercial terms in return for naming the yacht for the Race.
- On 10 April 1981 the bank refused to have its name associated with a sporting event visiting South Africa. Loan negotiations were ended.
- On 16 April 1981 I started to buy time from my previous sponsors at £50 per day with a new deadline of 27 April.
- On 20 April 1981 I accepted an offer of cash sponsorship of £60,000 from a prominent British company in exchange for their naming the yacht. I offered to borrow the £120,000 previously agreed from the finance house, whose marine manager was delighted with the arrangement.
- On 24 April 1981 the finance house claimed the naming of the yacht and threatened an injunction to prevent me from granting it elsewhere.
- On 25 April 1981 the new sponsors withdrew rather than risk any involvement in the bad publicity that was likely to follow the finance house's threat. The bank offered a new deal 'better than the one I had lost'. The finance house would be my sponsors, supported by the whole new arrangement.
- On 27 April 1981 the chief executive of the bank, acting as the principal of the new arrangement:

1   arranged a loan of £200,000 by his wholly owned subsidiary.

The chief executive acting for his subsidiary:

2   loaned £120,000 as a normal commercial loan;
3   loaned £80,000 interest free for one year, the future of the £80,000 to be discussed after this period and, 'provided I had been seen to use my best endeavours to promote the bank, the whole, or

certainly a substantial part, to be written off';
4   undertook that the bank would underwrite 25 per cent of the value of unsold berths at the commencement of the Race.

The marine manager of the finance house signed the loan agreement on behalf of the subsidiary.

Narrative

Throughout 1980 I had built an 80 ft racing yacht in a joint venture with a giant US corporation. A boardroom shuffle in Phoenix, Arizona, produced a new chief executive unsympathetic to his predecessor's support of a 'limey' yachtsman involved in racing events outside the USA. The difficulty was resolved in January 1981 by offering me a generous buy-out option, but I was required to meet a deadline for completion, of 16 April.

Following meetings with a senior officer of a banking group, I was persuaded into a loan agreement with a marine division subsidiary, against which my yacht was mortgaged and properties held as security. A substantial portion of the loan was the subject of a sponsorship deal in return for the naming of the yacht and associated publicity.

Additionally, to guarantee income necessary to promote the racing campaign, which it was intended should be generated by selling individual berths to sub-sponsors, an undertaking was given to underwrite the value of 25 per cent of any berths unsold at the commencement of the Race.

In February 1982 the joint general manager (currently chief executive) of the bank arrived in Argentina to rename the yacht for the parent bank for the final leg of the race home to England.

On 27 April 1982 the chief executive and his successor acting for the bank:

1   refused to discuss the future of the £80,000;
2   demanded interest on the full £200,000, threatening to seize the yacht if I did not pay;
3   refused payment of 25 per cent of the value of unsold berths;
4   refused payment for VAT demanded from me by the inspector as chargeable for services rendered to the bank;
5   refused payment for radio calls made for PR purposes;
6   refused discussion with the parent bank of its debts to me;
7   promised to help find alternative sponsorship;
8   promised to move the loan to the bank if I was unable to meet payments.

Being unable to fund litigation, I attempted to pay, and was up to date with payments at June 1983.

An excellent publicity return was produced, but the banking group changed its mind and decided to end its involvement with its subsidiary.

The parent bank asked me to allow it to rename the yacht for its own publicity for the final leg of the race home to England, then ignored a most dramatic homecoming. Its subsidiary claimed I had breached my agreement with it by renaming the yacht; it then reneged on its sponsorship promises, refusing to pay me the substantial sums owed to me.

I had the choice of entering into litigation, which I could not afford, or paying off a loan considerably in excess of the amount the bank's finance loans committee had declared before the race to be the maximum I could service.

Although, with difficulty, I maintained interest payments alleged due, the bank later demanded the repayment of the loan in full. I agreed to pay on condition that I had three months to do so, and interest payments would be rolled up for that period to enable me to refurbish the yacht to make it more attractive to a potential purchaser or funder.

I spent time, effort and funds on refurbishment and had the yacht billed as a star attraction at the Southampton International Boat Show, from which prime position I hoped to improve on the refinancing options I already had, which I had every right to do. The finance company were kept fully informed of my actions and intentions, which they acknowledged in writing. Having allowed me to complete my spending on the yacht, the finance company arranged its arrest by the Admiralty marshal, alleging arrears in interest repayments, and during the opening ceremony of the Boat Show the yacht was dramatically chained to a jetty in full view of the world's press. This event being well within the three months' period where it had been agreed to roll up interest, I was outraged – but I had no doubt as to the outcome of the law, the agreement having been witnessed and recorded.

I was concerned that a trial might take up to a year to obtain and, once my defence and counterclaim were made, all I could do was wait, because there was no move open to me to secure the release of my yacht before that trial, but I assumed the law must be capable of dealing with the implications of its actions.

Admiralty law allows for the release of the vessel pending the trial if the disputed debt is paid into court. My offer to pay the alleged overdue interest was refused, because by alleging it to be overdue the finance company were allowed to allege breach of the mortgage agreement and demand payment into court of the whole loan sum, which I could no longer raise with the yacht under arrest.

It was a great shock to discover that although I had no say whatsoever as to what happened to my yacht, which was entirely at the marshal's direction, the marshal had no responsibility to care for the vessel under arrest which, in spite of my protests, was simply allowed to rot. All my suggestions that I be allowed to operate the vessel under his supervision to earn income to fund maintenance were refused. Without income, I could not fund maintenance, and the finance company would not.

The inequity of the law was first established when I discovered that, although I was denied the use of my yacht, and therefore the use of the bank's money as a direct result of the action of the bank, I must still pay to the bank interest in full on the loan. Being denied the use of the yacht to generate income, I could not fund the interest payments.

On 30 June 1983 the finance company:

1   called a meeting 'to discuss the transfer to the bank of the loan currently being provided by the finance house';
2   refused to discuss the transfer of the loan to the bank;
3   demanded repayment of the whole loan;
4   agreed to roll up interest payments on the loan in return for payment by 30 September 1983;
5   agreed no action before 30 September 1983, which would frustrate my efforts to repay.

Timetable of legal events

• On 17 September 1983 a member of the subsidiary arrested the yacht, alleging as unpaid the interest that he had agreed to roll up.
• On 19 September the finance house agreed to lift the arrest.
• On 21 September the finance house claimed to have been over-ruled by the subsidiary and arrest was to stand.

The subsidiary:

1   refused to accept payment of overdue interest, but demanded payment of the whole loan, alleging breach of mortgage agreement;
2   refused to accept £40,000 for release of properties held as security which they valued at 'probably less than £20,000';
3   refused to heed warnings that the yacht would deteriorate and depreciate rapidly without maintenance;
4   refused to fund maintenance of the yacht under arrest;
5   refused proposals for me to operate the yacht under the marshal's supervision to earn income to be paid into court to fund maintenance;
6   refused to talk to me further.

Admiralty law denied me any say in the events concerning my yacht. This law decreed that I had to pay full interest on the loan, although it denied me the use of my yacht and therefore the use of the money.

Having created a situation where the value of the yacht was falling and interest was piling up, the bank was able to obtain the hearing of a motion for sale of the yacht *pendente lite* (before a trial). My yacht had been removed in pristine condition from the best-selling position in the world – the Southampton International Boat Show – and they now wanted it sold in drastically deteriorated condition 'under the hammer'. If, when sold in this absurd way, the yacht did not realise what I now owed, the bank could seize and sell my securities and pursue me to bankruptcy – and all before a trial.

Although the outcome of this motion was of crucial importance, witnesses were not allowed; it was purely an argument by counsel, who could fabricate what stories they pleased.

My way of life ended abruptly when my counsel rose to oppose the motion for sale and the judge told him, 'Before you begin, I will tell you whatever you say I shall order the vessel to be sold', and refused to be moved from that decision. A print-out statement from the finance company's computer showing arrears was adjudged sufficient to make the arrest 'proper'.

The loan, it was claimed, although always referred to as 'provided by' the finance company, had actually been made by a wholly owned subsidiary for which the finance company was acting as agent at the time. Although the agreement to roll up interest had been made by the finance company, represented by the same people who had made the loan, they had not on this occasion been acting as agent and the agreement was not binding on its subsidiary, which had carried out the arrest.

There are many grave implications, and several questions of trust and integrity, in such a disgraceful plea, but the judge dismissed all such argument as irrelevant, and on this legal technicality awarded the sale of my yacht, and also made a future trial irrelevant for my defence for the trial had admitted overdue interest, claiming it to be by agreement. The judge, in declaring the agreement not binding, had turned my defence into an admission of guilt. He refused permission to alter my pleadings to meet the surprising and outrageous separate entity plea and thus, without the opportunity to call a single witness or to produce evidence, I was sentenced to financial ruin. The only concession I obtained was to be allowed six weeks to rectify depreciation, at my own expense, so that a better sale price might be fetched and my debt lessened.

When I recovered sufficiently from the shock and despair to visit my yacht again, the rot and decay were heartbreaking. Dozens of craftsmen and hundreds of thousands of pounds *might* rectify the damage in six months, but what I could do in six weeks, penniless and unaided, was negligible.

Neither the bank nor the law would want to take the blame for the deterioration, and there was a way out for both – a lowered valuation at the time of arrest. The judge granted a request by the bank for a retrospective valuation. They came up with a *current* valuation of £200,000. 'The present value is £200,000', said the judge. 'Deterioration has occurred, but has been offset by lack of wear and tear, therefore the value when arrested was the same £200,000.' This was an absurd ruling, for there was no wear and tear under arrest to be offset, and the value, when arrested, must have been the current value plus massive depreciation.

Legally, the value of the rusted, rotted, moulding, neglected heap, with ruined deck and seized-up equipment and machinery, became the same as that of the pristine Boat Show star condition yacht. Legally, the finance company had been given a fall-back reason for the arrest of the yacht: that their security had been at risk. The judge and the finance company now had a common cause.

I was told that there was no effective right to appeal under Admiralty law; the judge would have to agree to an appeal, and if he agreed he would hear the appeal himself, as the only Admiralty judge.

The matter being purely financial, my counsel argued it should be heard in the Chancery Division, where the bank's own pleadings left them open to various allegations of banking malpractice. We initiated a Chancery action against the parent bank, the two subsidiaries and their common directors, asking that the loan agreement be set aside and judgement given on an equitable basis.

The bank's lawyers countered with another motion: that my action be set aside as showing no just cause. While this move may have been acceptable, their success in getting the hearing of their motion transferred from the Chancery Court to the Admiralty Court, to be heard by the Admiralty judge sitting as a Chancery judge for the occasion, was questionable and, even more questionably, they obtained the transfer as 'By Consent' though it was bitterly opposed by my counsel.

The Admiralty judge was now invited to decide, as an impartial Chancery judge, whether I should have an action against a bank group to whom he has just given, under the most questionable circumstances, all that I possessed.

It was counsel for the bank who introduced the suggestion of charade. 'To have a trial', he said, 'would be a charade, because even if he wins hands down, not a penny will come back to his company.' In its description of the justice available to me, it is an argument worthy of study – even if I win hands down, I will get nothing back, so therefore I should be denied a trial.

His complaint that my pleadings 'were merely facts and evidence strung together' also seemed strange until the judge obliged with the rules of the court, 'Facts and evidence . . . are not admissible'. Witnesses were not allowed either, so the outcome was a formality.

In summing up the judge said, 'It is too late to seek to undo the bargain because . . . that would be on the basis of returning to the status quo, but the money could not be repaid now, as is apparent from the other action'. It was not *me* who had disturbed the status quo, the bank had. It was not my fault the money could not be repaid now. It was entirely a result of the action of the bank, who would have been paid at the agreed time had they not arrested the yacht. Yet because this situation caused by the bank had arisen, it was ruled that I must lose and they would win.

The judge struck out everything of importance, but left a few minor things that kept the action open, but at the same time precluded my being able to continue it by reserving the right to award costs to date at any time he chose in the future.

It was cleverly done. He maintained the *sub judice* status, but at the same time effectively ensured I would not be able to continue with the action. I would be kept on the hook with the spectre of an award of costs against me whenever I obtained funds. He raised a laugh from the bank's lawyers, saying, 'He may win the football pools, or even be successful in the next Round the World Race.' The judge said he hoped I would accept an offer of settlement from the bank, which he considered generous, and an offer was handed to me across the court in which they offered to accept the yacht and the properties and not to pursue for costs if I would agree this as a settlement. I was advised by my counsel to accept as, although it would leave me penniless, it was the only way to avoid the rigo s of bankruptcy.

I found it difficult to believe this could really be happening since I was innocent of any default or misdemeanour. My only 'crime' had been to believe that the joint general manager of the bank and the chief executive of the finance company subsidiary had meant it when they agreed to roll up the interest. This was surely perfectly obvious to the judge and everyone in that court, and yet the only way to avoid bankruptcy was to concur with the giving of all I possessed to the bankers, who had behaved abominably towards me.

I haven't had one whole night of undisturbed sleep since that time. My mind still cannot accept what happened at the whim of one judge.

I met with my MP and complained of being treated unjustly. I wanted the right to a trial where witnesses could be heard, for I knew the bank's pleadings could not survive then. My MP submitted the facts to the Lord Chancellor. To my pleas for a trial, the Lord Chancellor replied he could not intervene in matters that were before the courts. 'It cannot be said too often that no litigant should try to bypass the course of justice by laying papers before the Lord Chancellor', he concluded.

Of the transfer of the hearing between the courts, he said the transfer document said it was By Consent, so it was By Consent. (It took me over a year to get the Chancery Court to admit that the transfer had not been By Consent, but by then my MP took the view that it would not be in my interests to disturb the Lord Chancellor again.)

The marshal had been given the yacht to sell in June, and in December he told me he would not sell it until the following spring. All this time, interest continued to compound against me at £100 a day, plus storage charges and all the other costs of maintaining the arrest, and there was not one thing I could do to alter this. At the start of the madness, I had a £450,000 yacht and four properties against a claim by the bank of £215,000, offset by the considerable sums it rightly owed to me. The yacht had already devalued to £200,000; by the time it was sold it would be worth £90,000, and I would owe £350,000 to the bank, plus enormous legal costs.

Now, according to the legal doctrine, I may not claim that the uncontrollable increase of my debt, with the passing of time, put me under pressure to settle, because I had the choice not to settle – and instead become bankrupt. Therefore if I do settle, I am deemed to agree the settlement to be just and fair. It is quite cruel. I can assure the lawyers who espouse this doctrine that, in the real world, the pressure to settle was very real.

I finally agreed to the proposed settlement, having first obtained a witnessed agreement by the bank's solicitor that the yacht would remain for sale by the marshal and nothing would be done by his clients to alter this. It was his suggestion that I should be able to pick up the yacht cheaply and salvage some pride.

Three side letters, from the parent bank and the two wholly owned subsidiaries, accompanied the settlement agreement. One subsidiary appeared under joint letterhead with the other and the only signatures were those of the two men who had agreed to roll up the interest.

The subsidiary 'owning' the yacht applied to sell it to its parent bank for £215,000, which I regarded as a ploy to close the marine division books and to prevent me buying from the marshal. I objected, and this application was replaced with one for release and possession, which I opposed in court. I had an agreement that the yacht would remain for sale by the marshal. It was a condition of the settlement; it was witnessed and had been confirmed that day by the solicitor's clerk who was in court. My case was perfect. Counsel for the bank pleaded he could see how the solicitor might have made the agreement, but he didn't really mean it. The judge demanded to know my current valuation of the yacht, which I gave as between £80,000 and £100,000. He gave me 21 days to bid £200,000, after which possession was given to the bank.

After some reparation, the bank sold the following year for £90,000 having refused a superior offer from me. In trying to raise funds to make this offer, I discovered I was 'branded' as a debtor in excess of £200,000 and that no financial institution 'could' lend to me. I cannot get removed from this debtors' list because officially its existence is denied, though it works so effectively that, even now, I cannot get to be a joint signatory on a cash-and-carry group charge card.

I have looked to the banking world for help. The letterhead of both subsidiaries had claimed membership of the Finance Houses Association. I sent them a copy letterhead of the subsidiary subsidiary (which had arrested the yacht and claimed to be a separate entity). The Finance House Association confirmed it to be a subsidiary of the other and added 'the notepaper is very old or something is amiss . . . [this company] gave up its banking status in 1979'. They were quite clear that the subsidiary operated only as part of its parent and was only a member of the Finance Houses Association in this capacity. They appeared disbelieving when I told them of the events in court, but I provided proof and suggested there had been a breach of the Finance Houses Association's code of conduct. I was informed that no action was possible because, since my complaints, the parent subsidiary had resigned from the Finance Houses Association. The Department of Trade and Industry declined to become involved, informing me that the regulatory authority for banks was the Bank of England.

I unsuccessfully sought a meeting with the Bank of England. I persisted, and eventually obtained the information that 'the authorisation criteria in the Banking Act require us to be satisfied that banks conduct their business with integrity, prudence and appropriate special skills'. I described, in the fullest details, my treatment by the banking group, only to be told many months later by the head of banking supervision, 'I have identified no grounds for action under the Banking Act'.

I tried again, asking quite clearly, 'Are you saying that, according to the standards required by the Bank of England, the officers of the bank and its subsidiaries conducted their business with me: (a) with integrity, (b) with prudence, (c) with appropriate special skills?' and again, I asked for a meeting.

The reply was no more helpful. 'I am afraid I have nothing to add . . . and in the circumstances, I do not feel that anything would be achieved through a meeting.'

The truth is that there is no will to achieve anything and I have no power to obtain an answer to my question.

Conclusion

My valuations of the yacht and warnings of deterioration have proved true. The bank's valuation of £200,000, and subsequent sale for £90,000, shows a 55 per cent depreciation on an already decayed yacht. How much greater must have been the depreciation on a yacht in pristine condition; yet even taking the same percentage figure over a similar period, the value at the time of arrest must have been £444,000. (I claimed £450,000.) Some £345,000 worth of yacht has been lawfully dissipated. The shareholders of the bank have lost several hundreds of thousands of pounds on the loan and legal costs because of a stupid action of arrest, and a refusal to discuss it with me thereafter. Losses to the taxpayer on legal costs and lost VAT are substantial.

Everything I pleaded in court has proved to be true. The essential legal technicality on which the judge gave everything to the bank, that the wholly owned subsidiaries operated as separate legal and financial entities, has been shown to be absurd. The retrospective valuation placed by the judge on the yacht at the time of arrest has been shown to be ridiculous. Almost everything pleaded by counsel for the bank proved untrue. The transfer of the hearing from Chancery to Admiralty was admitted to have been not By Consent.

Yet I have lost my properties, as well as my yacht, and all that it cost to establish my yacht charter business. I have lost my reputation and my peace of mind. The effect on my family has been devastating. I cannot borrow money to start a business again. Yet I was, and I remain, totally innocent of any fault.

It has been a long and difficult struggle even to begin to understand from the mass of legal documentation – which was my sole possession after the events in the Admiralty Court – how my ruin was contrived.

I have continued to try to find a solution within the law. Solicitors have shown great interest in the case initially, then have gradually backed off after many months of wasted time. My fourth firm has just followed this pattern.

Time is running out for me, and I am convinced the only way I may get this gross miscarriage of justice investigated is by obtaining sufficient publicity to gain inquiry, from the legal point of view, into how I could be ruined by the absolute power exerted by a judge and without the opportunity to have witnesses and evidence heard and, from the banking point of view, into how the regulatory authority can ignore such blatant misbehaviour by a high street bank.

I ask for help in obtaining an inquiry into:

1 the miscarriage of justice brought about by the administration of Admiralty law in this matter and the confusion between Admiralty and Chancery actions;
2 the failure of the system of court transcripts;
3 the failure of the regulatory authority for banks to take action or even to discuss the matter.

I need action to:

1 restore my reputation;
2 remove the 'listing' that prevents me borrowing money to start a new business.

Transcripts

To understand more clearly what had been done to me, I wished to obtain transcripts of the hearings. I assumed that, bearing in mind the importance of High Court judgements, transcripts would automatically be taken of all hearings and that the quality of recording equipment used would match the seriousness of its purpose. I was horrified to discover that it would cost me thousands of pounds to obtain 'full' transcripts of my hearings. I therefore tried to identify areas that I considered to be of crucial importance to my contentions of unfair treatment, with the intention of purchasing the limited material that I could afford.

I identified first an agreement between counsel to value the yacht at £300,000, later denied by the bank and the judge, but which I knew had been made during the very first court appearance. I was told that, although part of that day had been recorded, the section I needed had not. Similarly, a transcript was not available of the moment when the judge, in attempting to justify the increase in interest payments demanded by the finance company in respect of the subsidiary's loan, had declared: 'Clearly these companies are one and the same.'

I then turned to the final appearance in court when the judge had rejected what I believed to be my irresistible plea against release and possession by the bank. This was a hearing that both judge and counsel for the bank had remarked upon as being most unusual in their experience. Additionally, there was the unusual factor that I was representing myself in a High Court action, and there had been some quite remarkable exchanges with the judge. If ever a hearing needed to be recorded, it was surely this one. This hearing had not been recorded at all, I was told.

I established that there were transcripts of the 'Chancery' action, but I also knew they were incomplete and things that had made me very angry were missing. In the typed transcripts I bought, there were gaps where the recording was said to be inaudible, and they were annotated 'as approved by the Judge' who, as I understand it, is permitted to edit the document. I simply record what I discovered.

As an electronics engineer, I allege that the recording equipment in use was so worn and obsolete that it is unfit for use in matters that so gravely affect people's lives, and I do believe its use must lend itself to the supposition that it is not in the interests of the judiciary to make available accurate, reliable, complete and inexpensive records of hearings.

I am prepared to offer my services to the Lord Chancellor to design and oversee the installation of a system that is secure, inexpensive, continuously self-monitoring and cannot be compromised.

Useful addresses

Association of Brokers & Yacht Agents
Wheel House, Petersfield Road, Whitehill,
Bordon, Hampshire GU35 9BU
Tel: 0420 473862

British Marine Industries Federation
Meadlake Place, Thorpe Lea Road, Egham, Surrey TW20 8HE
Tel: 0784 473377

European Boating Association (EBA)
RYA House, 22–24 Romsey Road, Eastleigh,
Hampshire SO5 4YA
Tel: 0703 629962

General Register & Record Office of Shipping & Seamen
Block 2, Government Buildings, St Agnes Road,
Gabalfa, Cardiff CF4 4YA
Tel: 0222 586214

Lloyd's Register of Shipping, Yacht & Small Craft Services
71 Fenchurch Street, London EC3M 4BS
Tel: 071 709 9166

Motor Boat & Yachting
King's Reach Tower, Stamford Street,
London SE1 9LS
Tel: 071 261 5333

Royal Yachting Association
RYA House, 22–24 Romsey Road, Eastleigh,
Hampshire SO5 4YA
Tel: 0703 629962

Small Ships Register
Driver & Vehicle Licensing Agency,
Swansea SA99 1BX
Tel: 0792 783355

Yacht Designers & Surveyors Association
Wheel House, Petersfield Road, Whitehill,
Bordon, Hampshire GU35 9BU
Tel: 0420 473862

Index

Admiralty law 122–3
arbitration 20, 26, 109
arrest warrant 7–9

bailment 8–9, 27–8, 77–9
'betterment factor' 4–6
bill of sale 45, 66, 80, 82, 108
BMIF build contract 90, 23
boatyard estimates 21
boatyard liability 75–9
breach of contract 2–3, 24–5,
    82–3, 92, 119
British Marine Industry's
    Federation (BMIF) 109
  build contract 20, 90
British Registrar of Ships 55
British Tonnage Certificate 80
brokers 21–22
Brussels Convention 60
builder's certificate 66
building contract 90–4

caveat emptor 49
Certificate of British Registry
    55, 67, 80
Chancery Court 125
collisions 4–6
completion dates 19–20
Consumer Credit Act 1974 70
Consumer legislation 3
contracts 18–19, 24–6
  for the sale of a vessel, verbal
    63
  new build 2–3
  repair 33–5
'civil wrong' 22
classification certificate 13–17
Criminal Injuries
    Compensation Board 79
Customs & Excise stop notices
    66

damage to boat 7–9
  by boatyard 36–8
damages (financial
    reimbursement) 17, 25
  during towing 97–9

defects in new boats 2–3,
    110–16
design defect 101–5
double diagonal hull fault 85–9
'duty of care' 8, 14–15, 78, 88,
    87

Escrow account 18
European Community law 60

finance company liability 71
Finance Houses Association
    119, 128
fixed price contracts 18–19
fraud, suspicion of 51–4
fraudulent insurance claim
    55–7

General Register of Ships 45
Germanisher Lloyd-type
    certificates 117
Helpline, Motor Boat and
    Yachting v
High Court Judgements 131
  writ 76–7

indemnity insurance 89
Institute Yacht Clauses 4–5, 31
insurance claims 30–2, 36–7,
    52–4
insurance companies 4–6
  failure to honour claim 106–7
insurance policies, restrictions
    on 60
'insured peril' 102–5
International Maritime
    Organisation (IMO)
    59–60

keel, faulty 1–3

Legal Aid Board 54
'legal charge' 46
legal title 28
liability, insurance 7–9
'lack of due diligence' 74
legal protection insurance 117
liquidation 91
Lloyds insurance 60

Lloyds Register of Shipping 13–15
Lloyds Rules 13
loans by finance companies 69–71
loss adjuster 52

'market overt' 40
marine insurance *see* insurance companies
Marine Insurance Act 1906 74
'merchantable quality' 2–3
Merchant Shipping Act 1894 11–12, 45, 46, 64, 95
Misrepresentation Act 1967 22–23
Motor Boat and Yachting Helpline v

navigation lanes, obstruction of 99
negligence, 5–6, 8–9, 22, 31, 64, 72–4, 87–9, 97–101
new boat defects 110–16
notice of intention to sell 28

obstruction of navigation lanes 99

'perils of the sea' 53–4
personal injury claim 31
Portuguese law 58–61
private investigation 37
professional indemnity insurance 88–9, 104–5
proof of ownership 83

raising a wreck 62–3
Receivers of wreck 11–12
Receivers (liquidation) 93
Registrar of British Ships 47
recovering stolen goods 40–1
rejecting a new boat 25–6
right of lien over goods 34–5
Royal Institute of Naval Architects 89
Royal Yachting Association 92

Sale of Goods Act 1979 2–3, 21, 24, 36, 39, 40, 46, 49, 64, 70, 82, 87, 93, 104
salvage 10–12, 43, 63, 99–100
seaworthiness 112–18
secondhand boat, purchase of 107–8
Small Ships Register 40, 45, 46, 55, 57, 95, 108
Society for Underwater Technology 89
stage payments 18–19
standards of workmanship 24–5
stolen boat, sale of 39–41
stop notice, Customs & Excise 66
subcontractor's liability 91
surveys 1, 48–9, 67
  new boat 117
  Lloyds 14–15
surveyors 21, 36–7, 45, 85–9

Theft Act 1969 57
theft claim 53
third party claim 5
'tort' 8, 22
Torts (Interference with Goods) Act 1977 27, 40
towage contract 100

ULDB design 110
undischarged debt 95–6
Unfair Contract Terms Act 1977 2–3

VAT, liability for 66–8
verbal agreements 62–5

warranties 2–3
Whitbread race boat finance 119–30
write-off 52